WE
NEED
TO
TALK!

CREATING SPACE
FOR HEALTHY CONVERSATIONS
ABOUT SEXUALITY

WE NEED TO TALK!

CREATING SPACE FOR HEALTHY CONVERSATIONS ABOUT SEXUALITY

ADAM MEARSE, PH.D.

REDEMPTION PRESS

Published by Redemption Press, PO Box 427, Enumclaw, WA 98022

Toll Free (844) 2REDEEM (273-3336)

Redemption Press is honored to present this title in partnership with the author. The views expressed or implied in this work are those of the author. Redemption Press provides our imprint seal representing design excellence, creative content, and high quality production.

ISBN: 978-1-68314-507-3 (Paperback)
       978-1-68314-508-0 (ePub)
       978-1-68314-509-7 (Mobi)

Library of Congress Catalog Card Number: 2017960522

For Christina, who brings joy, passion, and organization to my life.

For Zachary, Elizabeth, and Jackson, my most treasured talking partners.

And, for all the students and parents that have allowed me to walk alongside you.

CONTENTS

INTRODUCTION

YOU HAVE PICKED up a book that claims it can help you create an environment in your home, church, friend group, etc. for healthy conversations about sexuality.[1] Good for you! If you read and follow the strategies offered within this little story, I believe that this book will live up to that claim.

I am thoroughly convinced that sexuality takes up more headspace in the minds of teens and young adults than any other single subject. Young people are inundated with sexual topics in entertainment, news media, at school, and certainly in their own thoughts. There was a time when parents and others who care about young people could simply drop a few hints, wink a couple times, and assume their kids were on the same page about sex and sexuality. Of course, that did not really work even then, but in an age where kids have nearly unlimited access to information, opinions, images, and video in the palms of their hands, parental silence is flat-out hurtful. It is time for parents, and others who care, to get in the game - and I believe this book is a good place to start.

Before you jump in, there are few things I want you to know about *We Need to Talk*:

1. It is about a plan. More than anything else, I want you to finish this book with a concrete strategy for creating space in your life and environment where sexuality is openly discussed and it is understood as healthy and important. As you read through each chapter, you will see that the Thompsons (the stars of our story) will create a plan of their own. In the back of the book, you will find space to create your personalized plan in the same manner. I genuinely hope you will take time to work through this. Add to, subtract from, and change it to suit your needs.

2. It is short. This is not because I do not have more to say about sexuality. My own kids will readily testify that I have a nearly unending stream of thoughts to share. This book is short because I want you, my much-appreciated patron, to read the whole thing. You are busy. You have jobs to show up for, households to run, and people you take care of. Research is startlingly clear that readers tend not to finish long books. I believe the ideas here can truly

help you and your family, so I desperately want you to get all the way through the book. Thus, brevity.

3. It is a story. I wrote *We Need to Talk* as a narrative for a couple reasons. Chief among them, I want you to read the whole book (I may have mentioned that already). My hope is that the story helps keep you engaged, and possibly even adds some whimsy to the process. Another reason for the format choice is that I want to offer you examples of people engaging in thought and conversations that really happen. In fact, the conversations represented here are based on those that I have had myself, or others have shared with me. This may be a good place to say that I patterned *We Need to Talk* after some of the works of Kenneth Blanchard and Spencer Johnson. Perhaps you've read *The One Minute Manager*, which they penned together. It is brilliant in its simplicity of format and depth of insight. Of course, they have proven to be brilliant thinkers and communicators, so their success in writing is no surprise. I owe them a debt of gratitude for both their impact on my own thinking as well as for the idea of writing this book in a similar style.

4. It has people in it. *We Need to Talk* tells the story of the Thompson family as they seek wisdom and strategies to help them make their home a place where sexuality is commonly and openly discussed. They gratefully receive insight from friends and family. None of these characters are real. They are all composites of people I know and have interacted with over the years. In some cases, characters are

a bit of an homage to individuals that have been particularly valuable to me, but none of them exist fully in the real world. Nonetheless, I hope you enjoy them.

5. There are endnotes. This book is based on research and established social-science theory. The intersection of faith and sexuality is my primary area of academic inquiry and writing, so some of the research cited is my own. Most of it is from other scholars in fields such as sociology, psychology, and communication theory. There are also a few notes tucked away in there just to offer a little more commentary (some of it attempting to be humorous) on statements or ideas included in the narrative. The endnotes are the extended conversation I would have with you if we were talking about this in person over a great cup of coffee.

NOTES:

1. Sexuality is a very broad topic. As an example, below is the World Health Organization's definition of the term. I include it here because, if nothing else, I want you to see how complex sexuality is and how much of our humanness is involved in it. If *this* isn't a topic worth quite a bit of conversation, I don't know what is!

"A central aspect of being human throughout life encompasses sex, gender identities and roles, sexual orientation, eroticism, pleasure, intimacy and reproduction. Sexuality is experienced and expressed in thoughts, fantasies, desires, beliefs, attitudes, values, behaviors, practices, roles and relationships. While sexuality can include all of these dimensions, not all of them are always experienced or expressed. Sexuality is influenced by the interaction of biological, psychological, social, economic, political, cultural, legal, historical, religious and spiritual factors."

World Health Organization. 2006. Defining sexual health: report of a technical consultation on sexual health, 28–31 January 2002, Geneva. World Health Organization. http://www.who.int/reproductivehealth/publications/sexual_health/ defining_sexual_health.pdf (Accessed September 3, 2014).

MEET THE
THOMPSONS

MARIA THOMPSON PULLED into the after-school pick-up line at Elmwood Elementary. Five-year-old Andrew, having returned home from kindergarten earlier, was singing along to the radio from his car seat behind her. Her daughter, Kayla, soon came scampering out with the rest of her second-grade class and climbed into their minivan.[1] As they pulled away from the curb, Maria absent-mindedly recited the same question she asked each day: "How was school today, Sweetheart?" Kayla's response changed the Thompsons' world forever.

"School was fine. Kind of boring. Mommy, what's sex?"

Maria felt like her heart stopped beating instantaneously. Trying to play it cool, she responded with, "What, uh…what do you mean, sweetheart? Where did you learn that word?"

"I heard some of the older girls talking about it. One of them said she wanted to have sex with some guy on You-Tube. What does that even mean?"

Maria's head was swimming. The steering wheel was starting to feel slippery from her sweaty palms. "Sex is… It's when… I'll tell you what, let's talk about that later, OK? I was thinking of stopping for ice cream, what do you say about that?"

The kids cheered as Maria pulled into the ice cream shop. She knew this was a total parenting copout, but Maria felt lost, more than a little terrified, and entirely unprepared.

Fortunately, ice cream was exactly the distraction Maria hoped it would be. Kayla was soon lost in the rainbow of flavor choices and the rush of sugar. To Maria's great relief, the word sex was not uttered again that afternoon.

William eased his truck into the driveway, glad to be home. Working as an electrical engineer for a local power company, he always felt mentally drained when he arrived home in the evenings. As he eased open the front door, he was looking forward to a hearty meal and a relaxing night. That was not to be the case.

His daughter Kayla and son Andrew were sitting on the couch as he walked in. Leaping up, Andrew ran headlong into his legs with a power hug and a shout of, "Daddy!" William hugged and tickled his son for a moment. Kayla looked up from her math homework and said, "Hi Daddy," with a smile. William absolutely loved that smile. He kissed the top of Kayla's head as he walked past her and into the kitchen. Hearing him enter, Maria turned from the chicken she was seasoning on the counter to face him. William knew immediately that this was going to be a long night.

"What's wrong?" he said. "You look mad. Or sad. Or, something."

"I am! All of those things!" Maria said, keeping her voice low.

"What happened?"

"Your daughter came home from school today and asked me what sex is!" Maria let that statement sit there for a moment. She somewhat enjoyed the stunned look on William's face — now he knew how she had felt earlier.

"What?" William half-whispered, half-shouted. "Where did she learn that word? Was it a boy? Which boy? I'll kill him."

"She heard it from some of the older girls at school," Maria replied. "Apparently one of them wants to have sex with someone on YouTube. I don't get the whole YouTube celebrity thing, by the way. But, we'll get back to that later."

William was silent for a moment, trying to process how the idea of sex ended up in the head of his precious, innocent little girl. Could he get it out of there? Was there a chance she could forget she ever heard it?

"What do we do?" he finally asked.

"I don't know," Maria replied. "I've thought about it nonstop since school let out. Maybe we should just have 'the talk' with her," she said, making finger quotes in the air.[2]

"Isn't she a little young for that?" asked William, doubtfully. "My dad didn't tell me about that stuff until I was fifteen."

"How'd that work out?" asked Maria, knowing full-well that William remembered that experience as one of the most awkward of his childhood.

"So, what then? Where do we even start?"

Maria thought for a moment, then had an idea. "What if we try to talk to some people about it?"

"Like who?" William asked cautiously.

"I don't know...how about Anita? She raised the best kids ever. She always seems to know what to do," said Maria, a hint of optimism in her voice.

"That's not a bad idea," said William. "You go talk to her. Maybe I'll swing by and see if Duane has any ideas."

"Your brother?" Maria asked doubtfully. "He doesn't even have kids."

"True, but he is a football coach, so he works with kids all the time, and he has a degree in psychology, I think.

Plus, he's good at figuring out tough problems…and this is a doozy."

"OK," said Maria, feeling a little momentum building. "You talk to Duane and I'll go have coffee with Anita. After that, we'll see where we stand. I don't think Kayla is too worked up about it. She doesn't seem to understand why it's a big deal. Hopefully, that will buy us a few days to figure out what we are going to say to her."

"Alright," William sighed. "If that doesn't work, can we just keep her home until she turns thirty?"

NOTES:

1. Fourth grade was the most common age cited by my own research participants as the age at which they became aware of sexuality as a force in their lives. However, I see this age dropping in casual observation. I interviewed college students, all of whom are in their mid-twenties as I write this book. In the years since they were children, the cultural saturation with sexuality seems to be driving this first-awareness down toward first or second grade. There were a variety of ways my interview subjects described this awareness beginning: jokes from older siblings, their attention captured by a romantic scene on TV, stumbling across something on the internet, and the like. Most of these were relatively innocuous experiences that served to make the subject consciously aware of sexuality for the first time they

could remember. This research was published in my Ph.D. dissertation, which can be accessed here:

Mearse, Adam. 2015. *We Need to Talk: Evangelical College Students' Perceptions on Positive Orthodox Sexuality and Pedagogical Implications for Church Leaders and Parents.* Trinity International University. ProQuest Dissertation Publishing.

2. "The talk" doesn't work. Research indicates it actually derails communication among parents and their children. Parents overestimate the positive effect it has on their children and generally feel overly positive about how the conversation went after it is over. Children, on the other hand, end up feeling embarrassed and awkward and never want to discuss sexuality with mom and dad again. Which, they frequently do not.

Regnerus, Mark. *Forbidden Fruit: Sex and Religion in the Lives of American Teenagers.* New York: Oxford University Press, 2007 (pg. 60).

CHAPTER 1

RELATIONSHIPS

ANITA WAS NOT simply a friend to Maria. She was more of a second mother. Over the past few years, Anita and her family had become an integral part of the Thompsons' lives. Thus, it was an easy phone call for Maria to make the next morning. She invited Anita to meet at a local coffee shop, the site of many hours of previous conversation between the two women.

Later that morning, they were sitting in the back corner of the shop with hot drinks in front of them. As with most Saturdays, the shop was bustling with activity. Fortunately, a couple was just leaving, so Maria and Anita laid claim to the over-sized chairs they had occupied. After a few minutes of catching up, Anita said, "Well, you obviously have another reason for asking me to come have coffee. I can see in it your eyes – you're stressed out about something. What is it?"

Maria fidgeted slightly, then started in on the story of the previous day. When she had finished, she said, "…and, that's why I'm here. William and I are at a loss for what to say to Kayla; how much to say; how to even get started. I was hoping you could help me. You have raised such great kids and I know you guys talk about everything together. It used to make me a little uncomfortable, but now I see the importance of that kind of openness. But, where do William and I even start to do that with our kids?"

"Wow!" Anita replied, with compassion in her voice. "Big day at the Thompson house." Both women laughed softly. "I am certainly no parenting expert, but I'll tell you a couple of the most important things we have learned about raising kids. Let's see…well, first, 'Go to the mattresses.'"

"That's from, *You've Got Mail*." Maria said excitedly.[1]

"Yes. So good, right?" Anita replied. "It's something of a battle cry. You are Kayla's parents and you must get in there and fight for her. It's a huge world with lots of influences – many of them are not what you want for your kids. You are the front line. You and William need to take charge and help Kayla and Andrew understand and work out sexuality. The kids will have more input coming at them on that topic than you can imagine. Everything from television to billboards to things they overhear at school, as you have already discovered. They need you. Right now. Not as spectators, as participants."

"Sure," Maria said, nodding slightly. "I just didn't expect this topic to come up so early on."

"Oh, sister, don't even get me started on how quickly time passes when you are raising kids. We live in a different world than it was even when you were young. Sex is absolutely everywhere in the lives of kids these days."

"Ugh! I hate that!" Maria said with lament in her voice.

"Me too," Anita replied. Then, looking Maria in the eye, she continued, "But that is the reality. There is no point arguing with reality. You should take on the attitude that you are going to be the one that helps your kids work through all the crazy questions they will have about their bodies and sex. You will be the filter for all the junk they'll hear, or think they hear, from everyone and every source around them. You and William must dedicate yourselves to becoming the first and most trusted source for information when your kids have questions about sexuality. If you don't, Google will, and I am pretty sure you do not want that to be the case."

"You're right," Maria agreed. "That's definitely not what I want. So, what do we say to her? How do we get started?" Maria asked.

"Well, that brings me to one of the other most important things I know about parenting. You might say it has become our parenting philosophy, though we've never really talked about it in those terms. In fact, you've seen it a hundred times at our house – it's on a large framed picture in the kitchen." Anita paused, giving Maria a moment to think about it.

"The one with the family walking down the trail in the woods?" Maria asked.

"That's the one. Do you remember what it says?"

Maria thought for a few seconds. "It's a Bible verse, right?"

Anita thought she detected a note of skepticism in Maria's voice. "Yes, it is. It's from Deuteronomy, chapter six. Now don't go dismissing it just because it's old or sounds preachy to use the Bible. Remember, you asked me what has worked for us as parents. This is it. Deuteronomy six. Look it up on your phone. You need to see it for yourself."

Maria was not a model Christian by any stretch of the imagination. Her Grandpa Lou was a minister until he retired and she and her family attended his church when Maria was a child. But, her parents had stopped making her go as a teenager, so Maria chose not to go. As with many young parents though, she and William had started to attend church again when Kayla was in preschool. They felt a sense of obligation to introduce their children to God. They had met Anita and her family shortly after they began attending. Over the past year or so, Maria had been surprised to feel a stronger personal connection to her Christian roots coming to life as well.

She pulled out her smartphone and opened the Bible app. She had installed it a couple years ago to keep from having to pack her large family Bible along with the snacks, toys, diapers, and other kid-related items needed to survive an outing with young children. It took her a minute to navigate to Deuteronomy six. "What part?" she asked, looking up at Anita.

"Read the paragraph that starts in verse four."

Maria scrolled down slightly and found it.

"Hear, O Israel: The Lord our God, the Lord is one. Love the Lord your God with all your heart and with all your soul and with all your strength. These commandments that I give you today are to be on your hearts. Impress them on your children. Talk about them when you sit at home and when you walk along the road, when you lie down and when you get up. Tie them as symbols on your hands and bind them on your foreheads. Write them on the doorframes of your houses and on your gates."[2]

Looking up, Maria said, "OK…so what do I do with this? Our kids already know the Ten Commandments. Isn't that what this is about?"

Anita smiled sweetly. "Think of this as going beyond just the recitation of commands. Think of it as talking about everything to do with life and faith – all the time and everywhere. A long time ago we decided to raise our kids with what we call an, 'as you walk along the road,' approach to parenting. We knew there would always be topics that we do not know enough about and decisions that are not black and white. We knew we would get a lot of things wrong and our kids would make a lot of mistakes. And, we understood we could not entirely avoid that and it wouldn't do any good to wait to start conversations with our kids until we thought we had all the questions answered in our own minds. We simply would never reach that point. Instead, we decided to concentrate on creating a home environment where we talk about everything as it comes up in real-life moments. We talked about sex when we know our kids had seen examples of it on TV or in a movie. We talked about it with the older ones when I was pregnant – the real process of making babies, the real body parts, all of it. We did it right in the moment – hundreds of short conversations over the years. No subject was out of bounds. We may not have had a great answer to all the questions that came up, but we assured our kids that we would figure it out together."

"Gotcha. That makes sense. So, did you guys ever have 'the talk' with your kids?" Maria asked.

"We never did, and that was on purpose. We have had a zillion conversations, but we never had 'the talk'. I don't believe in it. It makes it sound like there is just one block of information that you need to have packaged up and ready to drop in your kids' lap. I don't think it works. It just makes everyone uncomfortable and usually does not help kids at all. I think it makes things worse, really," Anita replied.[3]

"My mom and I had it when I was thirteen or so," Maria recalled. "It was about the most awkward thing ever. I remember thinking when it was over that maybe I knew more about sex than my parents did."

"I do not think that is uncommon at all. A lot of that is because assuming 'the talk' can work shows a limited understanding of communication. Remember that the point of talking with your kids about these subjects is not simply to transmit information. There are certainly some facts you need to tell your kids about their bodies and sexuality, but the most important goal as a parent is to help your kids make meaning of sexuality for themselves. Their biggest questions and concerns are going to be about what is going on inside of themselves – physically, emotionally, and mentally. Sexuality is such a personal component of life. Kids can feel very alone, no matter how much information they have about it.[4] Every person must work their way through it and you must walk that road alongside your little ones. It is not a one-night-in-the-kitchen proposition. It's a journey – sometimes confusing and even scary for them. They need you to hold their hand and help them process each experience and feeling."

"Huh," Maria breathed out. "That makes some sense, but I'm a little fuzzy on the not-about-facts-communication part."

Thinking for a moment, Anita had an idea. Leaning forward, she patted the surface of the coffee table in front of them and said, "It's a little like this table. You and I understand the fact of a table. It is made of wood…or some wood-like substance that Ikea invented. But, remember when we were here a couple years ago and little Andrew ran right into it? He cut his chubby little cheek a tiny bit."

Laughing at the memory, Maria said, "Oh goodness, yes. He cried forever. He was bent over chasing those cars he always had to have with him. If the barista hadn't given him that cookie, I think he'd still be crying."

"Exactly!" responded Anita, also smiling at the memory. "Andrew's personal experience of the table that day went far beyond the fact of a table. He learned some important personal truths about tables; that they are very hard; they are made of stronger stuff than he is; they can be dangerous. He also learned some things about himself. Namely, that his face is not a good part of his body to use when striking corners of solid objects."

"The point is, that day was not about the fact of a table. It was about Andrew understanding something about the table for himself. It was very personal to him. He did not need you to explain the form or construction of a table to him at the time, he needed you to help him make sense of his experience with the table in that moment."[5]

"OK," Maria said, somewhat hesitantly. "I see what you mean there."

Anita picked back up, "Every child feels like their experience with understanding sexuality, puberty, emotions

– all of it – is something no one else could possibly under-stand. And, in some ways, I guess that is true. It happens inside of each person. No one can know exactly what it is like for someone else. A parent's job is to help their kids talk through it all along the way so they can be as comfort-able as possible with their experiences, feelings, and ques-tions. The real goal is that between you and your kids, the communication keeps going, so you end up with a mutual, shared understanding about things they face. This allows your kids to feel like they can not only handle what's going on, but that you truly empathize with what they are dealing with as well. Most importantly, it shows them that you are entirely on their side in whatever they are going through. This kind of communication comes from a deep desire to see your child flourish as a person, not just an obligation to give them facts. It is hard work that will test your patience, but it will make all the difference in the trust and security your kids experience with you."[6]

After reflecting on that for a moment, Maria asked, "OK, so when did you start all of this, as far as sexuality is concerned? What age were your kids?"

Anita took a drink of her coffee. Setting it down, she said, "Well, that's one difference in the 'walk along the road' approach. There's no real starting point other than right now. We have always tried to talk openly with our kids. We started by calling their body parts by real names as soon as they could talk. I think if you make up pretend names for only certain parts of their bodies, kids get the impression that there is something weird about those parts. They passively learn that they are not supposed to talk about them. It's like on Harry Potter. Who's the old wizard guy?"

"Albus Dumbledore?" Maria offered, a little confused about where this was going.

"Yes! He tells Harry to call the bad guy by his name because being afraid of a name makes you more afraid of the guy…or something like that. I remember when I read that, I thought it was brilliant! So anyway, we called penises, penises, vaginas, vaginas, and so on. Real words for real parts of the body."[7]

Maria could feel herself blushing.

"I know," Anita continued, seeing the discomfort on her friend's face. "But, if your kids' bodies and their feelings about them are always a normal part of your family's discussions, it helps set the table for the more daunting conversations later in their teen and adult years. It teaches them that you and William are safe conversation partners and that their bodies are safe conversation topics. Start as early in their lives as possible, when stakes are low and kids have not picked up on the idea that their bodies and their feelings about sexuality are taboo. If you start young, then you have a chance to still be in the conversation when they go through puberty and have questions about intercourse and their own feelings about sexuality."

Anita paused briefly, taking a sip of her coffee. "It really is, walking along the road together. Most of it is mundane. It's talking about how their parts work. Talking about when their parts itch or hurt for some reason. It is everyday details and concerns. You let the conversations come up through natural moments of life, for the most part. The biggest step is just getting the conversation started."

Maria stirred her coffee absent-mindedly for a moment before asking, "But what do we do with Kayla? Based on what you said, we should have already been talking about her body a lot more and with very different words than we have used."

"You can't go backwards in life, sweetie. All you can do is start where you are. To start at seven is better than ten. Even starting at 13 would be better than 14. You don't have to make any major declaration to her, just be more intentional about saying body words and talking openly and without embarrassment – at least, don't show her when you're embarrassed. Talk about her body. Use real words for all her parts. Tell her that they are all good and have wonderful reasons for being there. It will be awkward at first and you may have to explain that she's too old to use pretend words anymore – and maybe you all should have been using the real words all along. Like everything else, the more you talk about it, the more normal it will feel. If you don't make a big deal about it, she will probably never even realize that you are shifting the way you speak."

"I suppose I could do that," Maria replied, a little skeptically. "I am not sure William ever could though."

"You might be surprised," Anita said, chuckling softly. "Men can also get used to talking about sexuality. It is important that he is part of the process too. There may be conversations that you want to have privately with Kayla, especially as she gets older. Woman-to-woman stuff. She will really appreciate those talks – although maybe not at the time. But, both Kayla and Andrew need to learn that these are not just girl discussions. They are normal. They are natural. We all talk about them because we are all sexual beings."

"He'll be delighted to hear that," Maria said smiling.

Laughing softly, Anita continued, "There's one more thing I would like to bring up."

"I'm not sure I can handle one more."

"Don't worry! This one really just goes along with the others, a supplement to them," Anita said. "Part of developing this kind of relationship with your kids is you and William opening up to them as well. Call it mutual vulnerability.[8] It makes sense when you think about it. You want Kayla and Andrew to believe that you and William understand what they go through – the good and the bad. The only way they can really believe that is if you share your own experiences, questions, and even failures with them. You want them to believe that, while you may not know exactly what they feel at any given moment, you have had parallel feelings and been through similar things yourself.

It gives you a sort of parenting 'street cred' with them," she finished, making finger quotes for emphasis.

Maria exhaled loudly. "Wow. I guess we have a lot of work to do. This is so overwhelming that I don't even have the energy to make fun of your use of street cred," she said, mimicking the gesture of air quotes.

"Maybe," Anita, smiled reassuringly. "Remember though, this is a journey. You do not need to go home this afternoon and spew sexuality-talk all over everyone. Just take it a step at a time. Talk it over with William. Make some plans and commitments about how you will get started. This is worthwhile work. You will walk together with your children through some of the most important experiences, feelings, and decisions of their lives. It is challenging, but it is the in-the-trenches work of loving your kids. You have a chance to help them make meaning of their bodies and minds – to help them grow into genuinely healthy people. Go to the mattresses!" She finished, with a bit of a dramatic flair.

After a brief pause, Anita had an idea. "You know who else you should talk to about this?"

Maria, feeling overwhelmed already, just raised her eyebrows in response.

"Talk to Bailey."

Bailey was Anita's daughter. Eighteen years old and a senior in high school, Bailey was considered an indispensable part of the Thompson family. She had babysat Kayla since she was a toddler. Kayla considered Bailey her best friend and Maria felt nearly the same way toward her.

"OK," said Maria. "Why do you think that will help?"

"Bailey can tell you what it was like as a kid growing up in our house. Maybe she has some pointers for you from the child's perspective. You know Bailey. She will be totally honest with you," Anita said cheerfully. "She'll tell you all the things we should have done better than we did."

Both women laughed and stood to leave, gathering up their belongings.

"That sounds like a good idea. I will get in touch with her later today. I want to think all this through a little bit first and maybe talk to William. We apparently need to get started right away," Maria said, leaning in to hug Anita goodbye.

Anita held Maria's shoulders for a moment and reassured her, "You will do great. Simply deciding to engage is the most important step to take." With that, the two ladies headed out the door to their vehicles.

Maria took the long way home so she could think through her conversation with Anita. A natural-born internal processor, she knew she would have to explain it to William and she wanted to sort it out in her mind before having that conversation. As she drove through town, some of the pieces started to fit slowly into place for her.

That evening was the usual controlled chaos at the Thompson home. Homework was done. Dinner was eaten and cleaned up. Stories were read. Teeth were brushed. What seemed like an eternity after the morning's conversation with Anita, Maria and William collapsed side-by-side on the couch. Despite her mom-exhaustion, Maria was anxious to tell William about her discussion with Anita.

"OK," she began, mustering her energy. "I need to tell you what Anita and I talked about today so we can be on the same page. There were some valuable ideas and I think it is important that we both understand them and decide how we will move forward."

"Alright," said William, sitting up slightly. "But give me the concise version. I'm not sure I can stay awake for more than that."

"Deal!" Maria replied, starting to feel some excitement about the conversation. "There is a lot to it, but as I drove home this afternoon…"

"Did you take the long way?" William interjected, with a knowing grin.

"Of course, I did!" Maria said, smiling. They both appreciated the value of a few extra minutes of silence in the car. "As I was saying before being interrupted," Maria continued with a wink, "driving home, I tried to distill it all down to some key ideas. This is what I have so far."

"First, I think the shock of hearing Kayla say the word sex shook us up a little. But, I think that's good. It impacted us so strongly because we know deep down that we have not done much so far to help our little girl understand sexuality."[9]

"She's seven years old!" William interjected with a bit of a groan.

"I know," replied Maria. "In a perfect world, maybe we would not have to worry so much about it, but this is certainly not a perfect world. Sex is everywhere. We all see it and hear about it constantly, right? It was only a matter of time before all the sexuality floating around out there caught up with Kayla. From now on, it's going to be on her mind more and more as she gets older. She needs us to help her process all the input, thoughts, and emotions."[10]

"Ooh…You are starting to go all mama-bear about this," William observed lightheartedly. "Could get fun!"

"Hey, these are our babies. We are going to be proactive about this. In fact, I think that's one of the first things I learned today. It goes on the list."

"There's a list?" William asked.

"Do you not know me but at all?[11] Of course, there's a list!" Maria retorted playfully. "There is always a list!" With that, Maria walked over to the desk against the wall. She picked up a pen, then riffled through a stack of papers in search of a blank page. She settled on one with a single line of blue crayon in the top left corner and returned to her seat next to William on the couch. Laying the page on the coffee table, she wrote:

RELATIONSHIPS

1. We are proactive.

"OK, we have the beginnings of a list!" William declared triumphantly. Walk me through it. Start with relationships – that seems vague," William observed.

"It's not vague, but it is broad," Maria replied. "Relationship is where it all starts. We have had it in our heads that we should come up with the exact right way to explain sexuality all at once – the words to say, the answers to questions, and all of that. However, that is not the best approach."

"We don't have to explain it? Great!" William said, with mock enthusiasm.

"That is not what I'm saying," Maria said, elbowing him lightly in the ribs. "We will get to what we say in a minute. What's more foundational is that we teach our kids that it is normal to talk about their bodies and sexuality. The most important thing for us is always our relationships with our kids. The goal of everything we do is to build trust and confidence in them."

"I'll buy that," William responded. "Keep going."

"Every child feels alone as they start to become aware of sexuality. Understanding these topics is such an internal and personal process. We cannot be content with our kids feeling isolated. We must create an environment where they feel comfortable talking to us about sexuality. That is much more important than whether we say the right things or can answer every question."

"Aren't we already concerned with all of that?" William asked.

"We are in theory, but not so much in practice. We are concerned with them, but we have not really done anything about that concern. Thus, number one on the list involves being proactive. We will take charge of our kids' knowledge of their bodies and of sexuality in general. We are going to help them learn to feel good about themselves. We will prepare them for puberty and for all they will hear about sex from all the junk that's out there. It's *our* job – no one else's."

"Oh, goodness," William sighed. "Does that mean we have to have 'the talk' already?"

"There is no talk," Maria said. She immediately held up her hand in front of William's face. "And, don't go into your whole Matrix thing right now. Stay focused!"

Feigning offense, William said, "Never even crossed my mind. So, what do we do?"

"That's next on the list," responded Maria. Bending over the paper she wrote the second line:

RELATIONSHIPS
1. We are proactive.
2. We communicate for meaning.

William looked silently at Maria, eyebrows cocked slightly in anticipation.

"We can be trusted with anything. We will show them that no matter what happens in their lives, we are the people that will walk with them through all of it. We will help them make meaning of it."

"Make meaning of it?" William interrupted. "Sounds kind of touchy-feely, psycho-babbleish."

"No. It's not like that. It's like when Andrew used to run into tables." Seeing the confusion on Williams face, Maria recounted the example Anita had offered her earlier.

After filling him in, Maria said, "Understanding sexuality may be the most personal experience anyone can have. When we talk to our kids, we will give them information sometimes, of course. But, passing on information is not the primary goal. The real goal is that they end up feeling like things make sense in their own minds. Until a topic makes sense and seems meaningful *to them* we keep working on it. We may have to come back to it over and over, but we will not quit until they have peace about whatever topic we are discussing."

"That sounds like a lot of work," William said. "But, it makes sense too. We do not want to be like old professor what's-his-name – the guy we had for econ in college."

"Professor Magister," Maria offered.

"Yes, that guy! Talk about someone who could spout off a lot of information without helping people understand anything." William paused for a moment. "Sorry, I got sidetracked. I definitely see the importance of communicating for meaning, though it will take some practice to get out of information-giver mode. You have anything else to add to the list?"

"As a matter of fact…" Maria said, bending over the coffee table to add a third entry to her list:

RELATIONSHIPS
1. We are proactive.
2. We communicate for meaning.
3. We "walk along the way".

"OK. Now you've lost me," William said, reading the new entry.

"I know," Maria replied. "It's from the Bible. Anita uses it. It's their parenting philosophy. Basically, it means that we teach our kids about sexuality in real time through normal life experiences. We call their body parts by real names. We answer questions when they come up. We start conversations when we know our kids have seen or heard something that may be confusing or new for them."

"So, we don't have 'the talk,'" William said, holding up finger quotes. "We have little talks all the time?"

"Exactly!" Maria agreed.

"But, we have to start using words like penis and vagina in real conversations?" William asked, with obvious trepidation in his voice.

"Yes!" Maria said with a reassuring smile. "You'll get used to it with a little practice. We need to talk about bodies and sexuality as part of everyday life, so our kids learn that those things actually *are* part of normal life. Conversation about these things is normal and expected. Then, when they get older and have bigger questions, hopefully they will trust that they can talk to us about those as well."

"I don't want to talk about all these things," William said, only half-joking.

Maria pointed back to the list and said emphatically, "It's our job! Our kids need us. There is too much crazy information and too many horrible images and videos out there. We will start small. We'll get better at it as we go along."

Leaning over to kiss his wife on the cheek, William said, "I know. They are our babies. We'll do this. We'll say the words and make the meaning. I really am with you. So, what's next?"

"I am going to have lunch with Bailey on Monday. Anita thinks she will have some helpful insights from a kid's perspective."

"That could be interesting," William replied. "I called Duane today. He can't get together until Tuesday. I gave him the two-minute version of what's happening. He sounded weirdly excited to talk about it."

"Great!" Maria said, gathering up the pen and the list. "I think we should plan to meet back here on the nights we have these conversations with people. We can share what we learn and add to our list."

"Ooh, more list-making fun. Let's do it!" William said, with a wink. Rising from the couch, he hugged Maria and kissed the top of her head. "I'm going to get ready for bed."

"OK," she said, giving him a final squeeze. "I'll put my list on the fridge and be right behind you."

As William walked away, Maria could hear him mumbling to himself, "Penis, vagina, penis, vagina, penis, vagina…"

NOTES:

1. Technically, this is a quote from *The Godfather*, which Tom Hanks' character cites as he describes "going to war" with little businesses like The Shop Around the Corner.

2. Deuteronomy 6:4-8

Holy Bible, New International Version. Grand Rapids: Zondervan, 2011.

3. I call this the "hand grenade" approach to communicating. Parents or church leaders throw something out there (a lecture, a book, etc.), then basically run away and take cover assuming the thing will do what they expect it to. Do not do this, my friends! It is ineffective and even counterproductive. Young people need to process information and make personal sense of it, not simply take in the facts.

4. When I asked respondents in my own research to reflect on their experience in coming to understand sexuality as a child, the most common theme that they expressed was a feeling of isolation. In speaking of her struggles with sexual temptation, Margaret (not her real name) recounted, "For the longest time it seemed like it was me alone, so I was kind of like, 'Yeah, I've got no one to tell.'" Another respondent,(not named) Ken, described his sense of isolation as particularly acute in relation to the onslaught of sexualized information coming his way as a teen. "It's confusing to have all these different perspectives coming from all these different directions and not really knowing at the time what to do with it." Sexuality is intensely personal. It is easy for children and teens to feel as though no one could possibly understand what they are going through. The more they can see others working through similar experiences and questions, the less isolation they will feel and the more readily they will engage in future discussions.

5. This is a remarkably simple description of an educational philosophy called Constructivism. To give you slightly more context, the philosophy has its roots in the work of Jean Piaget and others who help us understand that learning is a complex interaction of both external forces and internal processes. In the example of a toddler running into the table, the table is an external force. The toddler certainly learns about the fact of the table, but his experience also includes making meaning of pain, personal

weakness, the comforting role of his mother, etc. The table is not just an artifact in the world to him, it is a web of ideas, experience, and emotion. Sexuality should be approached this way as well. Our children's learning processes should be understood as a complex, life-long journey toward making sense of experiences and questions physically, emotionally, and spiritually.

6.   Somewhat related to constructivism, at least for this discussion, is Jurgen Habermas' groundbreaking work on communication theory. Habermas argues that much of communication is not just a linear process in which data is transfered from point A to point B. For example, if my wife sends me a text that reads, "Pick up milk on the way home," that is linear. Simple data transmitted from her to me. No interpretation necessary. However, if she sends me a text that says, "I'm unhappy," that is a very different kind of communication. Habermas helps us identify this mode of communication as a process that requires mutual meaning-making between two parties. The point of this type of communication is not information transfer. Rather, it is an empathic relationship of mutual care and trust in which the two parties commit to persisting in their communication until they understand each other and are both comfortable with where they end up on a topic. "Rightness" or "wrongness" are not usually paramount here - just understanding. Habermas' work on communication theory and philosophy is expansive and quite dense. As an introduction, I recommend:

Finlayson, Gordon. *Habermas: A Very Short Introduction*. New York: Oxford University Press, 2005.

If you want to dive all the way in, Habermas' full work is found in the two-part series:

Habermas, Jurgen. *The Theory of Communicative Action, Volume 1: Reason and Rationalization of Society*, translated by Thomas McCarthy. Boston: Beacon Press, 1984.

Habermas, Jurgen. *The Theory of Communicative Action, Volume 2: Lifeworld and System*, translated by Thomas McCarthy. Boston: Beacon Press, 1989.

7. Seriously, on what great problem of humanity can Albus Dumbledore not offer wisdom? The exact quote is as follows: "Call him Voldemort, Harry. Always use the proper name for things. Fear of a name increases fear of the thing itself."

Rowling, J.K. *Harry Potter and the Sorcerer's Stone*. New York: Scholastic Press, 1998.

8. Mutual vulnerability was a very common theme in my research. The college students I interviewed consistently stated, in summary, that for kids to feel comfortable talking about difficult topics of sexuality with their parents or other adult mentors, the adults needed to be open about their own experiences, questions, and failures. Mutual vulnerability between parents and children is a crucial building block required to establish enough trust and comfort for children to feel supported and understood.

9.   When their parents, churches, and so on, do not offer explicit teaching on sexuality, the implicit (unspoken, but understood by everyone) teaching is nearly always perceived as negative. In other words, when parents do not speak directly and honestly with their children about sexuality, kids naturally pick up on facial expressions, eye-brow raises, keywords, and tensions, which lead them to draw conclusions such as, "My body is dirty," or "Sex is evil." These messages are internalized and become very difficult to identify and overcome, even later in life when the child may be married or otherwise sexually active.

10.   Sexuality takes up more headspace than any other topic for young people. Men and women ages 18-25 think about sex between 140-388 times per day. While this study targeted emerging adults, I do not imagine an average high school student is much different. Teens are bombarded by personal feelings, hormones, discussions at school, jokes heard from friends or siblings, movies, music, and even the news. Topics and feelings of sexuality constantly stream through their mind - consciously and unconsciously. That being the case, failing to engage in these conversations is akin to psychological abandonment. Yes, it is that serious.

For the full study cited here, see:

Sex on the Brain? Fisher, Moore, and Pittenger; Journal of Sex Research 29 (2012): 69-77.

11.   "Do you not know me but at all?" A Phoebe-ism from the television show, *Friends*. That was for my wife.

CHAPTER 2

HONESTY

WHEN MONDAY MORNING arrived, Maria saw her kids off to school then headed to the office. An Associate CPA for a local accounting firm, her workload tended to ebb and flow with the end of fiscal quarters. This was not a particularly busy season of the year for her, so she was able to take an extended lunch and meet Bailey at one of her favorite cafés in town. Bailey ordered a chicken salad sandwich. Maria decided on a seared tuna salad. They found a table toward the back of the café where they began to eat their lunches and catch up on the past few days. When they had covered the news in each of their lives and the conversation lulled for a moment, Bailey decided to jump into the real reason they were together that day.

"So," Bailey said with a sly smile. "Mom told me what happened with Kayla."

"Yep," Maria replied, exhaling. "Suffice it to say, that threw us for a loop. We've been scrambling since then to figure out how to respond and what we need to do about all things sexuality going forward. You know me. Once I get started on something, I have to work it all the way through. So, we're pulling together all the voices we can muster in an attempt to get us going in the right direction. Your mom was a great a help, as always."

"Well, I don't know if I will be as much help as she was, but, I am happy to tell you what I know," Bailey said in her customary cheerful tone.

"I really appreciate it," Maria replied. "This popped up so suddenly. I feel like we're already playing catch-up here - and Kayla is only seven!"

Bailey finished swallowing a bite of her sandwich and replied, "Yeah, but at least you're getting moving now. All the major challenges are still ahead of her. You do have to catch up, I think, but not too much. She may not even notice."

"That is what I keep telling myself when I feel stressed out about all this," Maria responded. "Now, let me ask you a question. What do you think your parents have done particularly well to help you guys understand sexuality, your bodies, sex…all that?"

"Wow! That feels like a pretty serious question to answer with chicken salad in my mouth," Bailey said as she swallowed the bite she was working on and took a sip of her water.

"Yeah, sorry. I've been stewing over where to start since Saturday. I couldn't think of a smooth way to do it, so I thought maybe I would just put it all out there right off the bat. You can choose whatever parts you want to talk about. If this feels like an interview, I apologize. I'm not really sure how to have casual conversations about these things yet," Maria said with a quick wink.

Laughing slightly, Bailey replied, "No problem. Let me see." She paused briefly to take another bite of her sandwich. "OK, here's one. My parents have always been very open with us about all sexuality matters. Just really…honest. Maybe that's the best word for it. Honest."

"Interesting," said Maria, leaning in slightly. "That's a good word. Tell me about that. What was it like? In what ways were they honest?"

"Well, let's start with questions," Bailey began. "They have always encouraged us to ask questions and they have always been willing to talk about any questions we have. Sometimes they even ask the questions themselves, I guess."[1]

"What do you mean?"

"Let's say we were watching a movie – earlier in my teen years. If a sexual scene came on the screen, they would pause the film and ask if I knew what was going on in the scene, or if it seemed strange to me. To be honest, it was always a little awkward, but I knew they were serious, so we usually ended up talking at least a little. One time, we were downtown and ended up stuck in traffic because of the Gay Pride parade. It was so colorful and eye-catching. I was probably only 10 or 11 at the time. I asked dad about all the rainbow flags. We had a long talk about the LGBT community while we sat there in the car. That was one of the most important talks I think we ever had about sexuality - just sitting there in traffic."

"As you walk along the way," Maria quoted with a smile.

"Yep. That's their thing," Bailey said smiling broadly. "But, hey, it has worked pretty well. I think it is important for kids to know they can ask questions without getting in trouble or having their parents freak out about things. I once asked mom what the term gender dysphoric meant. I had heard it on a talk show, I think. She had no idea. But, she and I looked it up together and talked about it for a while. I appreciated that she was comfortable with not having the answer right away. I think that's fine too – parents' being honest about what they don't know and finding answers alongside their kids."

"Whoa! I would have no idea how to have that kind of conversation with Kayla," Maria said.

"I think it's one of those things where you cannot be ready to answer every question all the time. You just have it in your mind that you won't run away from any question that she asks. You'll do your best to discuss any topic and you will search for answers when you don't know them off the top of your head. Kayla does not expect you to be an expert on everything in the world. I think she just wants to know that you are going to help her figure things out."

Maria took a bite of her salad, taking a moment to process Bailey's words.

"Oh!" Bailey said with restrained exclamation. "That's another good thing my parents do, I think. You have to tackle the hard topics head-on. I remember when I asked my mom about gender dysphoria. In the back of my mind, I think I asked that question as a test. I knew that was probably a loaded word. I wondered if that would make her flinch. Parents can't run from the difficult stuff. Those are exactly the things kids need help figuring out the most."[2]

"Sounds like fun," Maria quipped.

"I can pretty much guarantee that your kids will ask questions that make you uncomfortable or make you feel like you don't know what you are talking about. I think that what my parents do so well is to make us feel like they are genuinely grateful when we ask questions like that – even if they do not know how to answer them right away. We can tell they really do want us to ask them about anything that is important to us," Bailey responded.

"Knowing your parents, I believe they really are grateful. I want us to be that way with Kayla and Andrew. It's a little scary though."

"Yes, it is," Bailey agreed. "But, that's kind of the point too. For me and my friends, the whole world of sexuality is a little scary. It's like, in some ways it is absolutely everything – your whole identity. On the other hand, for some of my friends, their parents or churches never talk about it at all – like it doesn't even exist. One of the best things you can do for your kids is to help them keep it all in perspective. You know what I mean? Help them keep their sexuality at kind of a normal, manageable size in their minds." As she spoke, Bailey held up her hands in front of her to indicate a spectrum.[3]

"Oh. Yeah. I see what you mean. If it's overwhelming for me, it will be even more overwhelming for my kids – especially as they encounter increasingly complex topics."

"Exactly," Bailey continued. "Help them feel like sexuality is something manageable. Most of that comes from just being open to talking about it all the time. You know how it is when you're a kid. The things that do not get talked about seem extra intriguing and you build them up in your head. You tend to either make more of them than they are, or you get scared of them and avoid them, ending up totally naïve. You don't want either of those things to happen."

"True," agreed Maria. "This is challenging stuff, but I think we can manage it."

"Good," Bailey said with a smile. "Because I'm not done yet."

"Oh," laughed Maria. "Great! What else do you have for me?"

"Well, I was thinking. Another way my parents have always been honest with us is in sharing their own struggles. I cannot remember a time when any of us kids struggled with a question, or even a behavior, where we didn't learn something new about our parents' lives and what they had experienced. Like when they first found my brother looking at pornography and my dad told us all that he had been addicted to porn for a while and what a struggle it was for him to break free of that. It really helps to know that your parents understand what you're going through."

"Ooh..." Maria grimaced. "That part doesn't sound fun. I can't imagine telling Kayla about all the ways I have failed or fallen into situations I should not have been in."

Nodding, Bailey replied, "I totally get that, and you do not have to share *all* the failures. Well-chosen examples will be enough. The thing is, when you are transparent with your own less-than-wonderful past, it helps your kids feel better about the things they struggle with or feel guilty about. You guys are going to have certain standards of sexual behavior for your kids, right?"

"Of course."

"If you have standards of any kind, at some point your kids will not live up to them. I know you'll forgive them, but if they understand that you had your dark moments too, they won't feel like screw-ups. You might check with my mom on this, but looking back, I think that has also helped my parents be more empathic with us. They are in the habit of thinking about their own experiences and sharing them with us, which naturally keeps the judgement vibe in check."

"That makes sense," Maria nodded. "Empathic is a good word, by the way."

"Right?" said Bailey excitedly. "I learned that in my psych class. Speaking of which, I have another psychology-type phrase for you. This thing we're talking about is what you might call, mutual vulnerability."

"Wait," Maria interjected. "Your mom brought that up when I talked to her."[4]

"Well, she stole that term from me," Bailey said with a smile. "It's a big deal when the people who should have the power, like parents, are vulnerable with the people who do not have the power, like kids. We watched a great TED Talk about the incredible power of vulnerability. I'll send you the link. You should check it out.[5]

"Very impressive! And, helpful. Chalk one up for high school psych class," Maria said with a laugh. "Vulnerability is not my favorite, but I definitely see the value in being honest about our own experiences with our kids. It is going to take some practice, of course. This is all very helpful. I feel like we are already heading in a positive direction. I cannot thank you enough for talking with me, Bailey."

"Great!" Bailey said cheerfully. Then, her face took on a more serious countenance.

"What is it?" asked Maria.

"Well, there's one more thing that I think belongs in this same category of honesty with your kids."

"Alright. Let me have it. We're invested now. I'll take anything you have to offer," encouraged Maria.

"I'm not really sure how to say it," Bailey began, somewhat timidly. "This isn't something I have even shared with my parents yet. My friends and I talk about it a lot though, and I think it's important."

"Go ahead, Bailey. You know you can tell me anything," Maria encouraged.

"It seems like there has always been a double standard when it comes to sexuality. For example, the last time we had talks on sexuality at church, the guys went in one room and talked about pornography and lust and some pretty serious topics. When they came out of those discussions you could tell that things had been emotional. My guy friends told me they were confessing sin, praying for purity and doing all kinds of important work. Meanwhile, the girls went into another room and we just talked about modesty and basically not having sex until we are married. I mean, the guys were in there digging into big topics and we were going on about how long our shorts should be and when it's appropriate to wear leggings. It feels like girls are still reduced to sexual objects and that our primary concern is to keep boys from lusting after us. We never talked at all about our own sexual desires or questions. You know that I have struggled with pornography and masturbation over the years. But, it's like girls are not supposed to talk about those things, even in a sexuality lesson! It feels like it's still too taboo for girls to take on these topics, but it's OK for guys.[6]

"Yeah, I remember that. William was one of the adults in with the guys. He said it was intense and very challenging for the boys," Maria offered.

"Right! The guys dealt with a lot of important questions and topics. The girls were essentially lectured on modesty – basically, just don't make guys lust, like it's our fault. And don't even get me started on the whole modesty idea! That's another discussion for another time," Bailey said, showing obvious frustration with the topic.[6]

"I guess what I'm trying to say," she continued, "Is that even when parents or churches do talk about sexuality, it seems that girls are treated more like sexual objects than sexual beings. It's as if our biggest questions and struggles are about clothes and what we are going to let guys do to us. I know a lot of girls that wrestle with heavy questions – porn, masturbation, really desiring to have sex. I think it's pretty common."[8]

"That's serious stuff," Maria said, leaning in slightly in a subtle show of support.

"I just thought," Bailey stopped short, looking for words. "If I'm going to sit here and give you 'parenting advice'," said with finger quotes and a smile, "I want to say that girls need to have access to the same support and teaching that guys have always seemed to have. We are sexual beings too! It needs to be acceptable for girls to bring up questions about sex and sexuality without being made to feel slutty. You know what I mean?"

"Definitely. I don't think anyone ever said anything to me other than 'don't do it!'" Maria agreed. "I guess it is still expected that girls do not think about sex that much and should not need to talk about it."

"Yeah, well I can personally guarantee you that that is not true," Bailey replied, raising her eyebrows slightly. "Really...not true."

"Gotcha. Thanks for including that. I don't know if I would ever have thought about it that way if you had not shared your experience," Maria said, as she gathered her belongings. "I need to get back to the office. You have no idea how much I appreciate this, Bailey."

"You are definitely welcome. Glad I could help. You know I love you guys and your kids. Thanks for the lunch." With that, Bailey leaned in to hug Maria goodbye.

That evening, Maria and William met back on the couch in their living room. The kids were in bed, at least for the moment. The couple sat together to review their day. It was a ritual they had subconsciously developed over the years – casual conversation on the couch while waiting to see who would wander out of bed for a drink of water, another trip to the bathroom, or to find a lost stuffed animal. Andrew was the only one to make an appearance, afraid he may have forgotten to kiss one, or even both, of them goodnight. He had not, of course, but they each gave him one more kiss and patted him on his way back to his room.

A few minutes later, the blissful peace that only falls over a household after the children are sleeping soundly became noticeable. Hating to disturb the tranquil moment, but wanting to process her discussion with Bailey, Maria said, "Well, I had another enlightening conversation today. I have a lot to tell you. But first, I will need my list!" She walked quickly into the kitchen to retrieve the same piece of paper she had used for their previous discussion. She found a pencil in one of the kitchen drawers and returned to the couch next to William.

"Alright, let's have it!" William said encouragingly. "What did you learn today?"

Maria picked right up. "It really comes down to one word – honesty. Bailey told me a lot of the wonderful things her parents have done to raise their kids. But, the thing that she said was most important is that they have always been honest about sexuality."

"That sounds, good. I'm with you so far," William commented.

"Well, wait for it," Maria said. "It's not just about saying things that are true. It is proactive honesty. We not only tell our kids the truth when they ask questions, we encourage them to ask, and even speak the questions that should be asked when they don't say them out loud."

"Huh. I guess you'll have to unpack that a little for me."

"Will do," Maria assured him. Maria wrote the word *Honesty* on the paper, parallel to the *Relationships* list. She underlined it and wrote the number one beneath. She paused a moment, searching for just the right words.

"I think the first thing on the *Honesty* list is that we love hard questions."

HONESTY
1. We love hard questions!

"With an exclamation point, huh?" William questioned.

"Always! We must create an environment that encourages our kids to ask questions about their bodies, sexuality, and other difficult topics. Not just the easy ones. They will have big questions and we need to be the people they bring them to." Maria explained.

"What if they don't ask us any big questions?" William asked.

"They may not, especially at first. So, we look for moments when they probably do have questions, but do not ask them out loud. If we see something when we are out together, or if there is a scene on TV - situations like that. They will learn that we are open to talking about the questions floating around in their heads. We need to show them that we are genuinely thankful when they do ask us questions - simple ones and hard ones." Maria said.

"OK, but what do we do when they ask something that we cannot answer? I'm certainly no sex expert. Although you might beg to differ," William said, raising his eyebrows.

"Seriously?" Maria said, elbowing him.

"Sorry, couldn't resist. It's so easy to make jokes when we talk about this."

"Well, try to focus, Fabio.[9] First, I think we have to make peace with the idea that that is definitely going to happen," Maria continued. "And we will be OK with those moments. We will be honest about our lack of knowledge. We will tell them we don't know the answer but we will figure it out together. We must not back down from any topic - even the ones that make us nervous. If we need help, we will find it. But, we cannot do the thing where we hide from uncomfortable topics and assume the kids will just get it as they grow up."

William nodded pensively.

"That brings me to another item on the *Honesty* list," Maria said, picking up the pencil again.

HONESTY

1. We love hard questions!
2. We practice mutual vulnerability.

"Nice word," William said smiling.

"It's from high school psych class," Maria said as she returned his smile. "You and I have to embrace the idea that our kids need to see us as imperfect, flawed, and trying to figure things out just like they are."

"I do not disagree that I am all those things," William began hesitantly, "But do we really have to tell the kids all the junk from our past?"

"Not all of it. And certainly not all at once," Maria said, patting William's back reassuringly. "But, we do need to make it a priority to share our own experiences – even some of the ones we are not proud of – when it seems to fit with what's going on in our kids' lives. They are going to disappoint us and make bad decisions. They need to realize that, while there may be consequences to those actions, we do not judge them and we genuinely understand their experiences."

"That sounds fun," William said with grimace.

"I don't think fun is necessarily what we're going for here," Maria said with a wink. "Speaking of things that will not be fun, especially for you…" With that, she bent back over the list and wrote the third line:

HONESTY
1. We love hard questions!
2. We practice mutual vulnerability.
3. Girls get to talk too.

"I don't get it," William said, looking down at the new entry on the list.

"Bailey brought this up, and I think it is very important for us to keep in mind. She and her friends feel like guys are treated as sexual beings, while girls tend to be treated more like innocent little flowers, just there to be looked at. We need to help Kayla talk about all the same things that guys usually discuss – pornography, lust, sex – all of it."

"You know, I have been in on some of those conversations with guys," William said with doubt in his voice. "They are not pretty. They're valuable, for sure, but very gritty. I cannot imagine having that kind of a conversation with Kayla. Also, if I find out that she is lusting after anyone, my brain might explode."

"I know," Maria responded. "But, this is a different age in the world. Kids have access to sexual content everywhere, all the time. We are careful with what we let our kids see, but the reality is that Kayla will eventually encounter all of it. We need to make sure we treat her like every bit as much a sexual being as we treat Andrew, so she will see as us allies when it comes to those topics as well."

"A sexual being? That's a terrible thing to say about my little girl!" William complained sarcastically. Slouching back on the couch, he moaned, "Are you sure we have to let her grow up?"

"I don't think we can stop it. But, we can help her grow up in the healthiest way possible." With that, Maria leaned back and laid her head on William's shoulder.

"Wow. I'm not sure how much more of this my brain can handle," he said, taking her hand. "I'm supposed to talk to Duane tomorrow. I hope he doesn't have too much to say."

Patting his knee, Maria quipped, "Honey, one thing I know about Duane is that he *always* has too much to say."

"You are right about that," William said. "I guess we'll do this again tomorrow night? Since I'm the one talking to Duane, I call making the list."

"Deal," Maria said as she gathered up the paper and pencil. "Just, don't mess it up." With that, she kissed him on the cheek and returned the paper to its spot on the refrigerator.

NOTES:

1. I teach at least one class a year to teenagers that is entirely driven by their questions about sexuality. I give everyone in the room a notecard and a pen and require them to write something on it and turn it in at the end of each session. This allows them to ask questions in total anonymity. They have scores of questions to ask when encouraged to do so. Some are basic anatomy. Some are ridiculously naïve or ignorant. Most are substantial and much more informed than you might expect. We must find ways to encourage our children and teens to ask questions so we can equip them with a biblical response within a Christian worldview. Even when they ask a question that you have

no answer to (and they will), you can earn their trust by working through it together.

2. The last young man I interviewed in my research was named Brian (but not really). We had finished the interview and as I packed my bag, Brian grabbed my arm firmly. He looked me in the eye and said, "If [parents and church leaders] aren't going to talk about all the LGBT stuff, you're just wasting our time." As we talked a little more, he communicated that young people do not need answers to the common questions about sexuality and faith. They crave honest discussion about the most difficult ones. They also realize that when someone offers simplistic answers to complex questions, that person is not a valuable talking partner.

3. I interviewed a young man named Richard (nope) who articulated this emphatically. He was adamant that churches and parents need to help young people right-size sexuality. When we create spaces for conversation and questions in our homes and churches, this is exactly what happens. Honest conversation prevents sexuality from being so overblown in our kids' minds that it overshadows every other part of their identity and thinking. It also prevents them from feeling as though they are supposed to ignore or suppress their sexuality. There is a middle ground here where young people can understand their sexuality as a vital component of who they are, yet not something they need to be enslaved to or overwhelmed by. Honest conversation helps uncover this space.

4. The repetition of *mutual vulnerability* in the first two chapters may seem accidental. I nearly removed it during editing, but it brings up an important fact - the themes presented throughout this book are not discrete. They build on and interact with each other. For example, I start with relationships in chapter one because every other idea presented in this book sits on a foundation of intentionality in our relationships.

5. Brené Brown unpacks the underrated power of vulnerability in her rather famous TED Talk. It is a high-level defense of vulnerability as essential to living the best possible life. She argues that vulnerability is an antidote to shame and puts us on the pathway to believing we are worthy of love and belonging. Those who press into vulnerability move toward lives of courage, compassion, and connection. These are important truths for our kids, particularly as we help them seek answers about their sexuality. You can join the nearly 30,000,000 viewers of Brown's brilliance here: https://www.ted.com/talks/brene_brown_on_vulnerability?utm_source=tedcomshare&utm_medium=referral&utm_campaign=tedspread

6. It is a common refrain among college students I speak with that young women in churches tend to be treated as though they are all but asexual and that the teaching they receive about sexuality is essentially a modesty talk. Abby (not really) told me in an interview that, "It bothers me that girls can't talk about [sexuality] for fear of being

seen as a slut." That about sums it up. We need homes and churches in which young women can openly discuss and wrestle with the myriad complicated feelings, desires, and questions that accompany female sexuality.

7. Modesty is a difficult topic for me and many other Christian folks. Some have been content to simply say that modesty means young women should not wear clothing that "makes" young men lust (helpless, hormone-crazed animals that they are). This understanding of modesty is not biblical, helpful, or healthy for young ladies, or young men for that matter. Modesty is a question of the heart and motivations – things that do not lend themselves to simple rules about inseam length. I wrote a blog series on where the conversation on modesty has taken us in the past few years. You can find it at: www.adammearse.com/home/2017/2/11/modesty-part-1-every-young-mans-battle-and-every-young-womans-problem

8. Pornography usage among women and girls continues to rise toward the level of men's usage. The Internet accountability site, Covenant Eyes, has pulled together important stats on the increase in women's porn usage here:

http://www.covenanteyes.com/2013/08/30/women-addicted-to-porn-stats/

9. Remember that guy? Fabio Lanzoni – romance novel cover model and *I Can't Believe It's Not Butter* spokesperson of the 80's and 90's. The most iconic shaved-chest and flowing hair of our time - for whatever that's worth.

CHAPTER 3

THE PROGRAM

WHEN HE GOT off work the next evening, William made the fifteen-mile drive to Lincoln High School, where his brother Duane had been the head football coach and humanities teacher for nearly a decade. William loved having his little brother nearby and always enjoyed visiting the high school to see Duane in his native environment. Duane was a bright student in his youth. He always made good grades and went to a great university after high school. He was one of those guys that never wanted to be anything other than a football coach. It was as though millions of microscopic footballs flowed through his veins. He loved the job and he was great at it, from what William could tell.

As he passed the locker room, heading toward the coaches' offices, William was struck by the familiar smells of high school. Each time he came to visit Duane, he experienced a mixture of nostalgia at the sights and sounds, along with a little bit of revulsion at the smells. He found Duane staring intently at game footage on the oversized monitor atop his desk.

"Hey there coach!" William called out, rapping on the door jam.

Smiling, Duane bounced up from his chair. William reflected that Duane was one of those people who seemed to bounce everywhere he went. Energy just radiated from him. "Hey, big brother!" Duane half-yelled. They did the three-pat bro hug that guys seem to do instinctively. "Great to see you!"

"Hard at work in here?" William asked, glancing at the monitor.

"Oh, you know how it is – always more video to watch. It'll keep though. Have a seat. Want a bottle of water or anything?" Duane asked as he walked over to the micro-refrigerator in the corner of the office.

"Sure," William replied, as he sat in the single guest chair across from the desk.

Duane retrieved two bottles of water and handed one to William. He opened the other for himself and took a long drink. He wheeled his captain's chair around to the side of his desk, so the two brothers could sit at a diagonal angle from each other. After a few minutes of conversation, in which they covered the latest activities of each of their children and the prospects for the Lincoln High football team's season, Duane broached the topic of sexuality in his usual enthusiastic manner.

"So, my sweet little niece asked you about sex, huh?" he said chuckling a little. "I would love to have seen your face when that happened."

"Well, she asked Maria about it, actually, so my reaction was second-hand. But, we did not see this coming. To be honest, we hadn't given it much thought. I certainly assumed that conversation was years down the road. We have made progress figuring out how we are going to move forward. Maria has had some good conversations with friends."

"Does she have a list going?" Duane asked, with a knowing grin.

"Naturally," William responded. He gave Duane a quick recap of the list and some explanation of what they had learned so far.

Duane said, "That all sounds great. You know, I've been thinking a lot about this since we spoke on the phone."

"Yeah, you actually sounded kind of excited to talk about it the other night." William said, eyebrows raised questioningly.

"Well, I was glad to talk to you in general, but I also think I have some ideas that might help with your particular dilemma." Duane responded, still smiling.

"Some of your psychology stuff? Or, coach stuff?" William asked jokingly.

"Actually, I was a sociology major, not psych. Those psych folks are too wrapped up with the inner world. That's not for me.[1] You never remember that correctly, by the way. Sociology and psychology are not the same thing." Duane chided. "You might say this is a little of both the sociology and the coaching. As you clearly do not recall, I became a sociology major because I thought it would help me as a coach – and it has! I knew I could learn X's and O's on my own. I wanted to study how groups of people function and how cultures are made. That is why I studied sociology… and, that is what I think can help you guys."

"Alright, Mr. Sociology-Not-Psychology, let me have it. Hit me with some wisdom." William encouraged him.

"Well, I am pretty wisdomous," he said winking.[2] Shifting immediately into what William recognized as coach mode, Duane leaned forward and continued, "What you guys need is a program – just like we have here."

"We need a football team?" William asked skeptically.

"That's the thing, there is a lot more going on around here than just a group of guys playing a game, right? We start with a goal - a vision. For us, the goal is to develop young men as individual leaders and mold them into the best possible football team we can muster. We want them to maximize their personal potential, then harness that within the structure of a team, which multiplies it so that the whole is much greater than the sum of its parts. That's what we try to do. That drives everything. Do you have a goal for your kids' developing awareness of sexuality?"

"As a matter of fact, we have been working on that. I would say it's something like, 'creating an environment where our kids always feel comfortable talking to us about sexuality' – that comes from the *Relationships* portion of the list." William said, with a look of satisfaction.

"Very impressive!" Duane responded with raised eyebrows. "That Maria really does do an excellent job keeping you people organized."

"For real." William said with a smile.

Duane picked right back up, "So, that's your goal. Now, how will you build a program to meet that goal? In other words, how are you going to create that culture in your home?"

"Aren't you supposed to tell me that?"

"As a matter of fact, I am. I am a sociologist after all!" Duane said triumphantly. "Think about what we do here. This is a football team. We play football, right? But consider all the parts that go into what happens on the field on Friday nights. We have the coaching staff, technology people, and athletic trainers. There a football field and people who take care of it year-round. There's a weight room, film room, and locker room and people who maintain those facilities. We have a tutor for guys that need academic support. This is a whole program – all of it focused on creating a culture of quality young men and a genuine team that we send out there to play football on Friday nights. What the players do during games is the result of a ton of other work, resources, and thought that happens off the field and all year long."

"Definitely," William agreed. "But, how does that translate into what we do with our kids?"

"Well, that is where sociology comes in, I believe." Duane responded. "There's this guy named Peter Berger, one of my sociology heroes. I love his work. He and Thomas Luckmann, wrote a book called, *The Social Construction of Reality*. It is an absolute masterpiece on the subject of creating cultures."[3]

"You're not going to make me read it, are you?" William asked with concern in his voice.

"No. Although, you should. I will give you the ridiculously simplified version of some of the most valuable concepts in there, given what is going on in your home. They are the ideas that I used to build my program here. I refer to them regularly as I evaluate what we do in our program."

"OK. Just take it easy on me. I'm a numbers guy, remember?"

"Yeah, yeah, I know. But this is really good stuff!" Duane said excitedly. "I have three ideas for you. They could even turn into a list for you to impress Maria."

"I like that!"

"The first is simple," Duane continued, "You need a team."

"A team? I thought Maria and the kids and I were the team." William responded.

"You are a team, but you need to think on a larger scale. You are the core, but the team must be bigger if you expect to pull off your vision of creating a culture that encourages your kids to talk to you openly about sexuality. You said your vision is to create an environment, right? It's the same thing, really. A culture is built when a group of people agree that certain ideas and values are worth holding onto, and they establish methods to maintain and strengthen those ideas over time."[4]

"OK. So, what kind of team do we need for helping our kids understand sexuality?" William asked, with a confused look on his face."

Duane continued, "You need people who are in this with you. People who want the same things you and Maria want for the kids; who have the same values you do. Think of it as a support system. The more people that the kids have in their lives who believe and speak the same way about sexuality, the stronger it will make your message. They need friends, mentors, relatives..." Duane paused briefly to point at himself. "…people who are on your team. Also, you need to verbally ask them to partner with you in this. Do not assume someone is on your team. Recruit them. Remember your *Relationships* list? You have to be proactive in team-building as well."[5]

"Gotcha. We need a team. That goes on the list." William said as he made a writing motion in the air. "Actually, that should be pretty easy right now with all the people we have already had conversations with in the last few days."

"Great! Keep in mind, you will have to make changes to your team as the kids grow. Kayla will form relationships with new people as she gets older that you will want to bring onto the team. When Andrew gets older he may require a totally different set of people. I regularly evaluate the people who influence my football players and whether those influencers still have the impact we need from them. Likewise, you will need to pay attention to the people who influence your kids along the way and consider bringing in new recruits as appropriate. When they have a youth pastor or a teacher they seem close with, you need to consider asking that person to partner with you."

"Huh." William said, considering this. "What exactly do we say to those people?"

"Keep it simple. Tell them you have this vision for your kids' lives, which includes other adults who will influence them in the same directions you and Maria are working toward, especially with your beliefs on sexuality. Ask that person if they have similar beliefs and whether they are willing to talk with your kids about it if the situation arises. That way, you are certain of a specific group of people who track with your values. Then, you can guide your kids toward them as ideal people to talk to about life."

"OK. I probably should have written that down, but I think I have the idea."

"Sure, you do! Plus, it will depend a lot on the person and your relationship with them. Just be plain-spoken and honest when you talk to them. This team we're talking about for your kids, is actually a mini-culture of its own and can be very strong in the face of our broader, western culture. It's like your team is a David going up against our highly sexualized western culture with all its images and ideas that promote having sex as often as possible and with every person you can find – that's Goliath."[6]

"Gotcha!" William responded. "Our little team is a tiny culture going against the larger culture – media, the Internet, all that. Right?"[7]

"Right! Pull together your team," Duane continued. "Ask them flat-out to be part of this mini-culture you are creating. That's the first part. Next up is your messaging. On our team we have sayings like, 'Hard work always pays off.' That is just one of several mantras that we repeat day after day. It's even printed on our summer practice t-shirts."

William grinned and said, "Please tell me you are not going to suggest I make t-shirts that say, 'We always talk about sex!'"

"That may be a little aggressive," Duane said laughing. "But, what you and Maria definitely need to do is to develop ways of consistently speaking about sexuality - things you will say over and over again. Maybe, 'You can *always* ask us,' or 'Mom and dad fear no question!'"

"Ooh!" William exclaimed, "I actually might put that on a t-shirt!"

"If you decide to do it, I have a shirt guy," Duane said with a nod and smile. "Berger and Luckmann call these, 'legitimations'. They are the things you say that constantly reinforce your most important values."[8]

"As in, they make your values 'legit?'" William asked, clearly proud of himself.

"Well, Berger and Luckmann might cringe to hear you state it that way, but if it helps you, go for it!" Duane replied. "This is hard work though, not just slogan-making. You and Maria need to have many conversations about the foundational values you want to instill and how you can keep those messages in front of your kids. You say them. You teach your kids to say them. You use them until they become inside jokes within your family. The other adults on your team say them – or at least say things that communicate the same values. In your case, legitimations are intentional ways you speak of sexuality and relationships with your kids, that help build the culture of openness and trust that you desire. This language continually communicates your core values."

"Got it," William said. "All jokes about making t-shirts aside, that really does make a lot of sense."

"Great! I have one more for you. Berger and Luckmann also use the term, 'plausibility structures'…and that's the next big step in shaping your mini-culture. Plausibility structures are the activities and traditions you incorporate into your life in order to reinforce your message," Duane said, leaning in a little to emphasize the gravity of the concept.[9]

"They make our values seem 'plausible,' I assume?" William asked.

"You're brighter than you look!" Duane joked, with obvious pleasure. "Now remember, you're trying to create a culture – an environment in which your kids can always communicate with you about sexuality and you and Maria are able to successfully pass on your values."

"Yep," William agreed.

"Those ideas and values are different in some ways than the values that your kids may find in places like movies and the Internet, right?"

"Definitely!" William said with enthusiasm.

"Then, for your values and ideas to trump those of the Internet, you need to make sure that you are providing structures in your life that constantly reinforce them."

"How's that different from the last one – the legitimations?" William asked.

"It is similar," Duane agreed. "Plausibility structures and legitimations go hand-in-hand. The difference is that plausibility structures are the things you *do* and the legitimations are your message – things you *say*. For example, you and Maria could commit to each reading one book per year on some sexuality topic, to increase your own knowledge base. You could establish a rite of passage where, when they hit puberty, you do something special to welcome each of your kids into the next phase of their lives. Perhaps you commit to a form of regularly checking in with your kids about questions that are going through their minds. It will take some creative thinking on your part. Somehow, you need to install practices into your lives that will perpetuate your ideas and values. Reinforce what you believe with what you do."

"Huh," William said, clearly thinking it through.

"Think of it this way," Duane offered, "The Internet, movies, and other influences will always be there. They will always be making a plausible case for an anything-goes view. If you want your kids to accept a different view of sexuality, you are going to have to provide constant reinforcement to help them see that your values can work – to help them accept those values as true and doable. You need consistent people, messaging, and actions that all work together to create the kind of environment you desire and to present it as viable option for your kids. Because, ultimately, they have to choose whether they will accept your beliefs or not."[10]

"See, that's that part I don't like," William said. "Why can't they just blindly accept that every word we speak to them is true?"

"That would be nice, right?" Duane said chuckling a little. "But, they need to become healthy people and that does require them to learn to think for themselves."

"I suppose," William said with mock frustration. "Anything else?"

"I think that is probably enough for now," Duane said. "If you guys can get started with these tasks, it will help you to create a real system that ultimately leads to a new culture for your kids and your home."

"Alright," William said, as he stood up. "Thanks, Coach! I always appreciate your insight."

They embraced again and Duane said, "Always good to see you, big brother. Hug the family for me. We'll have to get everyone together soon."

"Sounds good," William replied. "Good luck Friday night. We'll come watch the game next week when you guys are back at home."

"Great! I'll save you some seats."

William turned and made his way out of the locker room and back to his car. He was excited to offer Maria his list later that evening - so much so that he did not even take the long way home.

That night after they put the kids to bed – then put them to bed again – Maria and William sat down together. This time they opted for the kitchen table instead of the couch. Maria sipped on an iced tea. William had a glass of water in front of him, though he showed little interest in it. They caught up on their respective days at work for a few minutes. Maria shared that there was an incident at Andrew's kindergarten that day involving a group of boys, Andrew among them, deciding to hold all the classroom blocks for ransom until one of the girls shared the pack of candy she brought to school with her. The standoff was ultimately resolved peacefully, but some extra discussions on sharing and personal property had to be interjected into the day.

When that conversation had run its course, William was ready to jump into the review of his talk with Duane. "I'll tell you what," he started, "That Duane really does know some things. He's great with people. Oh, and he was apparently a sociology major, not psychology."

"Of course he was. Why can't you ever remember that? Never mind, what did Coach Sociology have to share with you?" Maria asked with a smile.

"For that, I'm going to need the list," William said as we walked ceremoniously over to retrieve it from the refrigerator.

"Oh, yay! I was hoping you would have a list!" Maria exclaimed with honest excitement and a noiseless clapping.

Returning to his seat, William placed the list on the table in front of him and immediately added a third category next to *Relationships* and *Honesty*. He wrote:

THE PROGRAM

"Alright," Maria said, encouragingly. "Tell me about 'The Program'."

"Alright. In short, what we want to do is create a culture of our own – one that values open conversation and instills our sexual values in our kids. It's a lot like creating a football program, at least as Duane describes it."

"Oh no!" Maria said, rolling her eyes back in her head as though dying. "Not sports stuff!"

"I'll leave the sports out of it," William said in a conciliatory tone. "But Duane really does tie them together well. Our system has numerous parts. It's not just about a conversation or two, as we have already decided –it's bigger than that. Similarly, it is bigger than just me and you and the kids. We need to think about how we can create an entire little culture of our own, which includes people, teaching, activities – all of it. We need to think big-picture and create a strategy for pursuing it."

"Alright. That sounds good. Where do we start?" Maria asked.

William picked up his pencil and wrote the first entry on his list.

THE PROGRAM

1. We have a team.

"First, we think about who is on our team. Obviously, there are the two of us. But, we need to be…" William paused and pointed to the first entry on the *Relationships* list, "…proactive about it. We are going to recruit people to help us with this. We have had conversations with Anita, Bailey, and Duane already. I think it is safe to say that they'll be on our team. We need to confirm that with them – to ask if they are willing to help us with this."

"I like it!" Maria said. "It's a little weird asking someone to be on your sexuality team, but I think this is important enough to get a little weird."

"Exactly!" William agreed. "We want trusted people to surround our kids with the same support and same values about sexuality that we offer them. We want to help Kayla and Andrew make friends who have similar values as they grow older. We will also probably need to pull in other adults and mentors that they connect with later in their lives. I was thinking we would conduct an annual review of our team. In fact, we should probably do that with all these lists."

"The annual review is a good idea. Maybe we could make a little parents' retreat out of it! So, yes, we'll put together a team. Can we get uniforms?" Maria joked.

"Actually, there was some talk with Duane about printing t-shirts. Oh! That brings me to the next item on my list," William said as he added a second item:

THE PROGRAM
1. We have a team.
2. We have consistent messaging.

William continued, "We need to have consistent messaging with our kids. Things we repeat over and over again that reinforce our values."

"Like slogans?" Maria asked, with a trace of doubt in her voice.

"Maybe," William replied, "But not necessarily. What we are aiming for is to decide on specific ideas that we want our kids to remember about sexuality and our family values. We will generate creative ways to repeat those things often. We don't always have to use exactly the same words, but we do always want to communicate the things that we believe are of central importance. We are battling to offset the messaging of the broader culture. For example, the most common narrative of TV or the Internet is something like, 'Have as much sex as you can all the time.' We need to provide them with alternative messages that affirm our values. Maybe something like, 'Sex is a great part of being married…after you're forty years old.' But we need lots of talk – about values, our relationship with them, communication, all of it. Maybe, 'Mom and Dad *love* hard questions!' could be another one."

"Um, I'm not sure they'll go for that one about waiting until they're forty, but we could give it a go. The 'We love hard questions!' one is a keeper though." Maria interjected with a grin.

"We'll have to work out the particulars, I guess," William said, winking. "The point is that our team needs to have consistent messaging for our kids that keeps our values in front of them all the time – from us and from the other members of our team."

"OK. That's pretty solid too. I believe Duane really does know what he's talking about," Maria said.

"I know! Though, technically, I think he stole it all from a guy named Berger." William replied. "Time for the last entry on my list." William wrote the third entry:

THE PROGRAM

1. We have a team.
2. We have consistent messaging.
3. We have consistent practices.

"To review," Marshall went on, "We'll have a team — a group of people all on the same page with our values and dedicated to helping our kids. And, we will have some things that we consistently say to keep our values in front of our kids. The final step is to create some practices that help reinforce them as well. Talking is good, but we need to be intentional about doing some things that reinforce our message."

"Like what?" Maria inquired.

"Some of them can be simple. Maybe you and I decide that every time we watch a movie with our kids we'll talk about any relationship or sexuality topics that may have come up during the show. Or, we decide that we'll read at least one book per year with our kids about relationships or sexuality."[11]

"Right! Those things seem doable. I guess we will work some of those out as we go. That will require a whole new list!" Maria said with enthusiasm.

"You bet." William replied. "Another idea Duane brought up is to add some kind of rites of passage for our kids."

"That sounds a little tribal. Give me an example."

"I was thinking about this on my way home. Maybe when the kids turn 12 or 13, you or I take them out on a date. We can talk with them about what it means to have feelings for someone else and how to make smart decisions about people they may want to be in a relationship with. Something like that." William suggested.

"Ooh, that's pretty good! Much less creepy than I was picturing in my head."

"Yeah. And, maybe we can create a tradition for when they get their first cell phones. We make a day of it. We go out to eat, let them pick out their favorite case…all that stuff. Then, we talk to them about the boundaries we are going to put on their phone usage and why having a phone is such a big responsibility. We will definitely talk about pornography, sexting, and what to do if they come across it."

"Wow! That is impressive. Way to go, Duane."

"Excuse me," William said with a look of great offense. "That one was all me."

"Then you, my dear, are even smarter than you look." Maria said, patting his hand affectionately.

"Why do people keep saying that?" William said with a posture of deep reflection.

"Alright!" Maria said enthusiastically. "This is great. Nice work today, Honey."

"It was kind of fun, really. I am starting to feel good about what we are pulling together from our conversations so far." William responded. "So, what's next? Who else can we talk to?"

"I had an idea about that. It's a little outside the box," Maria said, pausing for effect. "What if we go to talk to Grandpa Lou?"

"Your grandpa?" William asked with obvious surprise. "I did not see that coming."

"Well, he and grandma were married for over fifty years, so he must know something, right? I also think it might be good to gain the perspective of someone from another generation. He is so wise and thoughtful and knows all about the Bible. Plus, he's always fun to talk to."

"Definitely," William agreed. "I just hadn't thought in that direction at all. Let's do it. Maybe we could go see him together. We can have Bailey come watch the kids."

"Perfect! It's like a date…where we ask my septuagenarian grandpa about sex," Maria said with a playful cringe. I'll call Grandpa Lou tomorrow and set up a time."

NOTES:

1. I say this with the utmost respect, having completed the necessary hours for a degree in clinical psychology myself, only to decide at the end that I did not have the emotional fortitude for full-time therapy. Go see a therapist!

2. Joey Tribbiani! I could not resist one more *Friends* reference. I am done now.

3. I really cannot recommend this book strongly enough if you work with groups of people. It is relatively

short and not as difficult to read as you might expect a self-proclaimed treatise on social theory to be.

Berger, Peter and Luckmann, Thomas. *The Social Construction of Reality: A Treatise on the Sociology Knowledge.* New York: Anchor, 1966.

4. This is a definition I cobbled together based on the influence of thinkers, such as Berger, Luckmann and Andy Crouch. Speaking of Crouch, if you have not read his beautiful work *Culture Making,* put it on your "to-do" list. Not the pretend list that you will do when life stops being busy and you are rich, but the one where you go buy a book and read it as soon as you are finished with this one.

Crouch, Andy. *Culture Making: Recovering Our Creative Calling.* Downers Grove: IVP Books, 2103.

5. In my research with college students, they repeatedly mentioned the value that mentors had played in their lives. There are some conversations that kids need to have with people other than their parents. If there is an adult you trust and with whom your child has a relationship, recruit that person to be on your team. Another valuable product of having mentors in your children's lives is this: Very often your child will most want to tell *you* what they think about, struggle with, and how they have failed. But, they will need another adult in their lives that they can do a sort of test-run with. This has been a huge part of my life as a youth minister for the past 20 years. Students share things with me that they truly want to tell their own parents. Once

they say the words out loud and realize the world did not implode and that I did not react with shock and judgement, they start to believe that they can tell their parents as well – which they nearly always do.

6. Gathering a relatively small group of people who believe and practice something different than the broader culture (the counter environment, as Berger and Luckmann refer to it) is a phenomenon that takes place all the time along religious, ethical, and preferential lines. This smaller environment, such as your family or church, may share some of the same values as the dominant culture, but it is dissimilar enough that its members delineate the differences and believe them to be worth maintaining. For example, your family probably has particular views on sexuality and sexual behavior. If they are anything other than, "Have as much sex and experiment as widely as possible!" they are different than the dominant culture that we live in. We want to think of our families and homes as their own mini-cultures going against the larger, counter environment.

7. Another pre-eminent sociologist, Christian Smith, describes what he refers to as *subcultural identity theory.* The gist of it is that subcultures such as families or churches have values that clash against the wider culture in which they exist (i.e. The United States). These subcultures can have a remarkably strong influence on their members that outweighs that of the wider culture by establishing an us-versus-them mentality. This is not a hostile view of the

wider culture, but gracious delineation of important differences in values that gives the subculture's members a sense of clear identity, a rationale of their values, and even pride in their distinctiveness. When these conditions exist, subculture members are strengthened and galvanized against the wider culture. Smith describes this as the strength that is at the heart of evangelical Christianity's historic success in the United States. In thinking of our families and churches as subcultures, we can leverage the same kind of strength in our identity as people who know a better, healthier way of relating to each other.

Smith, Christian. *American Evangelicalism: Embattled and Thriving.* Chicago: University of Chicago Press, 1998.

8. Too many parents never go as far as legitimations. They do not clearly define their values, nor do they communicate them often enough for them to take root in the minds of their kids. Our children see, hear, watch, and talk about hundreds (thousands?) of ideas about sexuality every day. If we want our sexual ethics to withstand the torrent of other noise, we must be intentional about keeping our message in front of them.

9. Plausibility structures are the things you *do* to reinforce what you believe. Plausibility structures, for our discussion, may include such things as: reading one book a year with them about sexuality or relationships; creating rites of passage as your children turn 13, 16, 18, and so on in which you have intentional experiences and conversations

about dating, sex, etc.; developing the habit of stopping movies during sexual scenarios to say a quick word about it; choosing specific movies to watch with your kids that bring up topics to discuss; and annual youth group teaching series on relationships and sexuality. Anything you do that helps prop up your message and values falls into this category. The important thing is that you consciously choose to include such activities in your environment.

10. More sociology. Berger and Luckmann speak of externalizations and internalizations. Externalizations are ideas that come from outside of us – from others, television, friends, etc. What we work toward when we think about our families as mini-cultures is to help our kids see our values as intellectually and morally plausible, as well as practically legitimate – they lead toward a healthy way to live. When our kids start to accept our values as their own, the externalizations become internalizations – beliefs they own and claim for themselves. This is the goal! But, it only happens if we provide them with consistent messaging and activities that reinforce the messaging.

11. There are approximately nine gazillion books you could choose on this topic for every age of child. As your child reaches puberty and starts to think seriously about relationships, may I recommend a book that I believe every teenager and parent should read together? It's *Real Relationships,* by Les and Leslie Parrott. It has been updated recently, but I started to use this resource with teens over 15

years ago and it has proven to be the most valuable book on all aspects of self and relationships that I have come across. I have read it with both my older children as they hit their teen years. Check it out.

Parrott, Les and Leslie. *Real Relationships: From Bad to Better and Good to Great.* Grand Rapids: Zondervan, 2011.

CHAPTER 4

GOOD NEWS

MARIA CALLED GRANDPA Lou the next morning. Not surprisingly, he was delighted at the idea of having her and William over for a visit. They decided to get together on Saturday morning. The idea of waiting several days to have this next conversation nearly drove Maria mad with anticipation. However, as William reminded her, going to work was also important. When Saturday arrived, Bailey came over to spend the morning with Kayla and Andrew.

"Take all the time you need," Bailey encouraged.

"Yeah, take your time!" exclaimed Kayla, all too happy to spend as much of the day as possible with her best friend.

William and Maria stopped for coffee on the way to Grandpa Lou's house – always looking for a chance to sneak in a little treat on the occasion they had some time alone together. They made it to Lou's house around half past nine and rang the doorbell. After a few moments, Lou pulled the door open and greeted them with a warm grin. "How's my favorite granddaughter?" he asked enthusiastically as Maria hugged him.

Lou was in his late seventies. His shoulders stooped slightly with age and he walked slowly, with the help of a cane. He wore khaki pants and a white golf shirt beneath a burgundy cardigan sweater. On his feet were socks that featured unicorns and rainbows. He shook hands warmly with William and closed the door behind them all.

"Nice socks you've got there, Lou." William remarked with eyebrows raised.

"Thank you," Lou responded with obvious pride. "A man needs to have a little something to show his personality. I got these for my birthday from Miss Jennifer."

"Oh, how sweet!" said Maria. "How is Miss Jennifer?" Miss Jennifer had been Lou's secretary in his years as a minister. Maria remembered her as the one who always had snacks stashed away to share with her and her siblings when they went to visit Lou at his office.

"She's doing just fine. You know Miss Jennifer – always looking out for me. She decided I needed new socks last time she stopped by to drop off lemon bars. Oh, I do love her lemon bars," said Lou, clearly lost in that memory for a moment. "Anyway, can I get you two anything?"

"No thanks, Grandpa," responded Maria. "We stopped for coffee," she explained, raising her paper coffee cup as evidence.

"Never understood why people pay $5 for a cup of coffee," Lou replied with a slight waive of his hand and a grin. "But, if you're happy, I'm happy. Come in and sit down," he said as he ushered them toward the couch. Lou took a seat in his recliner facing them.

"So, what are we going to talk about today? Of course, I am always happy to have you two stop by for any reason. When I spoke to you on the phone, though, I got the distinct impression that this is more than just a social call."

Subconsciously taking hold of William's hand, Maria replied, "Well Grandpa, we've had something come up and we are really working hard to deal with it as well as we can. We have spoken with a few other people, but thought we would get your perspective as well, since you're so brilliant," flashing a toothy grin.

Sitting forward in his well-worn chair, Lou said with an inviting smile, "Well, this does sound interesting. Don't keep me in suspense, sweetheart."

Maria began to recount the events of the past week, beginning with Kayla's utterance of what they had come to refer to as, "The Question." She succinctly outlined the input they had received from Anita, Bailey, and Duane.

When she finished, Maria sat back a little, as though she had released some great weight she had been carrying.

William patted her on the knee reassuringly and both waited for Lou to speak. After what seemed like ages, Lou grinned mischievously and half-whispered his question, "You came to talk about sex, did you?" He chuckled lightly before saying, "Well, I didn't see that one coming."

"Believe me," William responded, "We didn't see it coming either. Then again, we have found ourselves in numerous unexpected conversations in the last week. We both admire your marriage to Maria's sweet grandmother. Maria tells me you used to do a lot of marriage and family counseling and were never afraid to talk about sexuality, even back then. We thought you would be a great source of wisdom for us. As you can probably tell, we are taking this seriously and trying to think about it from several different angles. While you know we haven't always been the most faithful church-goers, we do want our kids to understand sexuality in a godly way, as long as that does not mean they end up thinking sex or their bodies are evil or dirty or anything like that."

"Ah, well there's the real crux of the thing," interjected Lou, showing obvious excitement about the conversation. "That's where so many Christians and churches have gone off the rails in the past. In our attempts to keep kids from having sex, we've ended up making them think that sexuality is a bad thing and that their bodies are evil.[1] Those ideas are nothing like what the Bible tells us."

"Yes!" Maria exclaimed. "That is exactly what we want to avoid with our kids. We want them to see sexuality as something good and healthy. Can that even be done in a Christian way?"

Chuckling again, Lou leaned back in his chair. "Oh yes, my dear. I dare say your grandmother and I figured out a positive thing or two about sexuality in our day."

"Grandpa!" Maria chided. Then, looking at William, "I told you he'd have way too much fun with this."

"Sorry, sweetie!" Lou replied with a failing attempt at sincerity. "Couldn't help but toss that in there. In all seriousness though, the Bible is a definitively pro-sexuality book. There are obviously a lot of prohibitions in there, but the big picture of how sexuality fits into God's good creation is quite beautiful and compelling. If you ask me, Christians spend far too much time discussing why people should not have sex and not nearly enough talking about the undeniable picture of human flourishing that the Bible describes when addressing sexuality."

"Whoa!" remarked William with an impressed smile. "You hit your preacher stride really fast on that."

"Well, this is something worth talking about!" Lou described. "So, let's see…where do we start?" he said pensively. "Let's come at it this way. We will talk about some of the positive statements the Bible makes about sexuality, then maybe some things parents, churches, and others need to do well when it comes to teaching and living out those ideas. That sound good?"

"That would be great!" said Maria as she and William both nodded.

"Alright," Lou said as he stood up slowly from his chair. "First things first. You can't talk about sexuality without cookies." With that, he padded off toward the kitchen.

"Cookies?" William asked, casting an inquisitive look at Maria.[2] She just shrugged and they both waited. A couple minutes later, Lou returned carrying a plate of Oreos, which had been dumped and semi-arranged into a pile.

"Your grandma never let me eat these when she was alive, but I figure I might as well enjoy them now. At my age, what's the worst that can happen?" he said, winking mischievously at Maria. "Now, where were we?" he asked to no one in particular, as he found his seat. "Oh yes, you asked your grandfather about sex. I mean, sexuality."[3]

"Yes, Grandpa, sexuality." Maria responded with feigned annoyance. "Not that you forgot that in the last couple minutes."

"That's true my dear," he said smiling at her, "I just enjoy saying it out loud."

"Of course you do."

"In all seriousness though," Lou began, adopting a business-like tone himself. "There are some surprisingly positive statements about sexuality in the Bible." With that, he reached toward the end table near his chair and picked up a Bible that looked as though it would crumble to dust even as he held it. He opened its yellowed pages toward the beginning and began to smile broadly. Maria knew he was mostly holding onto the book out of comfort and appreciation – he practically had the entire Bible committed to memory.

"Sexuality has been part of God's good creation from the very beginning. The creation story itself has many important insights for us. Right off the bat, God shows that our sexuality is connected to our role as partners in his creative work – which is humanity's primary vocation. He says that we bear his image together as male and female. He did not say this about Adam when he was wandering around by himself. Only when male and female were present together – that is when God said, 'Here is my image.'"[4]

Maria pulled up the Bible reading app on her phone. For the rest of their conversation, she toggled back and forth from there to her notetaking app.

"I know there is a lot said and questioned these days about gender, and a great many important conversations to be had about it, but God saw the presence of male and female together as a full and good expression of his image."[5] Lou paused for a moment to take a bite of a cookie.

Wiping crumbs from his lap, he continued, "...and that little tidbit comes right in the middle of the big one – the creation mandate!" he said with growing enthusiasm. "God tells us that humanity was made specifically to partner with him in the ongoing work of creation. We are supposed to be stewards of the world around us – to help roll creation forward over time. Of course, we're also supposed to make more humans.[6] It would have been a pretty short experiment without sex, right?" he joked, looking proud of himself.

"God, in His wisdom and goodness, gave us sex so that we can do our part to keep creation going. That is certainly not the only reason sex exists, nor is sex the most important part of the creation mandate. We cannot be reductionists about either of those things, but that simple truth should not be overlooked either - by having sex and making babies, we do participate in the ongoing creation work of God. That is a big deal. I might also add, a pretty nice way to do our part. A lot better than pulling weeds."

"Amen to that!" William interjected.

"Yeah, well you guys have never given birth. That part isn't so nice." Maria chided, with a challenging glance at each of the men.

"Oh, very true, my dear. But you know, that was not supposed to be the case. Having children was not originally so difficult. All that pain is a byproduct of sin entering the world," Lou responded sympathetically.[7]

"But, there's also Genesis 2!" he continued, regaining his momentum.[8] "Adam goes to sleep and God creates Eve. When Adam wakes up, he declares, 'bone of my bone and flesh of my flesh!'" With this, Lou raised his arms up in a sign of triumph.

"For the first time, Adam realizes that there is someone enough like him to really get him. I believe that when he says, 'flesh of my flesh,' he was in awe of what a gift it was that this new creature clearly looked like she was of the same tribe as he was – unlike all the other animals he had just given names to. But then he also says, 'bone of my bone.' I think he sensed that they could connect on a deeper, soul level – something that feels like it is in his very bones. What a glorious description of how sexuality contributes to the deepest and most meaningful relationships we can ever experience."

"Wow, that is good." William said, exhaling.

"Oh, it gets even better!" Lou continued. "God then declares that a man will leave his father and mother and the two would become one flesh. This is sneakily pro-woman text by the way, but we'll discuss that another time.[9] The two-becoming-one is the real miracle here. God, who just claimed that he was making male and female to bear his image together, now says that through their sexual relationship and lifelong marriage, they can experience something like the mutual love of the Trinity. Just as the Father, Son, and Spirit are distinct, but also inextricably one, he declares that a married couple can experience a similar union. Couples are made to maintain their individual value and identity, but also to draw so close together that, somewhere along the way, they can no longer tell where the one stops and the other begins. I lived this with your grandma, my dear. There is nothing more sacred or mysterious in human relationships – in all creation – than this."

As he said this, tears welled up in Maria's eyes at the memory of grandma. She whispered, "I know you did, Grandpa. Your marriage was the most beautiful thing I have ever witnessed."

"There is no other relationship on the planet that offers such an approximation of the relationship that the Trinity enjoys. Sexuality and sexual intercourse are right at the heart of it. If ever there was anything to declare good in creation, it is the invitation to mirror the Father's relationship with Jesus and the Spirit. A biblical view of sex is not primarily about all the times and ways you shouldn't do it. Much more, it is about the beautiful, compelling vision for what sex helps accomplish in the right context. When sex is held in that high regard, there is nothing else that compares with it." Lou leaned back in his chair as though to catch his breath. The three of them sat in silence for a moment, reflecting on what Lou had just said.

Bolting up in his chair with a sly grin, Lou exclaimed, "Oh and we can't forget Genesis 2:25! That's the best line in the Bible!"

"Well don't keep us in suspense, Lou, what is the best line in the Bible?" William asked, leaning toward Lou in anticipation.

"They were both naked, and they felt no shame." Lou said with obvious satisfaction.

After a moment of awkward silence, they all began to laugh out loud. "You just like it because you get to say 'naked,'" Maria teased.

"Well, I will not deny enjoying that fact," Lou replied. "But there's more to it. We were created to enjoy our physical bodies. In an ideal world (which, we do not live in, of course), my grandbabies would never have any thought that their bodies are something to be ashamed of or are any way dirty. They should feel that their bodies are perfectly suited for their lives. I guess none of us can get away with feeling entirely shameless about our bodies, and I am not suggesting we develop some over-inflated sense of pride either. But, our physical bodies are also good. They are intended to bring pleasure and beauty and redemptive power into this world. I know so many people that grew up in churches and walked away with the idea that their body is evil. It is awfully difficult to change your mind about that when you get married and sex is instantly supposed to be beautiful and pleasurable."[10]

"Yeah, I guess that's true," Maria remarked. "It wasn't a real problem for us, but I have girlfriends that really struggled with sex when they got married."

"Happens all the time," Lou replied. "So, parents and churches need to find a way to balance their ideas of modesty with the fact that our kids need to grow up knowing their bodies are part of God's good creation."

"We definitely want that for our kids. It's going on the list," Maria said.

"The list?" Lou inquired.

"There's always a list." William said, before he realized he was saying it out loud.

"Oh, and make sure you say something about how good it is to be single." Lou blurted out, as though the idea had just struck him.

"What do you mean? What about being single? I thought the church wanted everyone to get married and have kids," William quipped.

"I know it can seem that way. Sometimes I guess it truly is that way. But, consider the fact that modern kids are starting puberty earlier and getting married later. Even young people who follow the absolute average arch of life are going to be single for a couple decades after they hit puberty. So, even pragmatically, we need a better theology of singleness."[11]

"Wow, I hadn't really thought about it that way," William said with obvious concern in his voice. "That's a long time to not have sex."

"Well, that statement is part of the problem with how many of us have historically spoken of and thought about sex," Lou picked up. "Most of what we communicate about sex is 'don't do it.' But, there is a lot more to sex than avoiding it and a lot more to singleness than trying to fix it by getting married."

He continued, "Paul tells individuals that they should stay single if possible.[12] Singleness allows people to offer their whole attention to partnering with God in blessing the world. Single people are agile – they can pick up and go where and when there are needs to be met in ways that married people and parents simply cannot. They can teach the church about what it looks like to have a heart that finds fulfillment in God alone. Consider this – if someone called you for help in the middle of the night, you would have to make plans for taking care of your kids before you could respond, right? Maria, if you felt a call to move to an orphanage in Africa, you would need to negotiate that calling with William, decide how to respond, figure out both of your jobs, address the kids' schooling…a thousand details. A single person could be on a plane to Africa tomorrow. If single believers can be shepherded to offer their hearts and lives to God as a unique gift of single life, singleness can be a season of great fulfillment and development. Faithful single people should also be held up as examples of whole-life devotion for others to live up to. Singleness is not for everyone forever, but it is for most people for quite a while. We ought to be casting a robust vision for living well as single people."

"I have certainly never considered singleness as an opportunity," William said. "Married guy's bias, I suppose."

"Well, today is the day to start deciding how you want to frame singleness for Kayla and Andrew when they start to become aware of sexuality in their own lives. Help them see it as a time of special focus on their relationship with God. Encourage them to be bold and to engage with big problems in the world."

"Whew! That's a lot to think about Grandpa," Maria said with a prolonged exhale.

"Yep, and we are not quite done yet," Lou responded, reaching for another cookie.

"We're not?" Maria asked.

"No, my dear, not yet. There are a couple more things that absolutely must be part of a Christian view of sexuality. The first is grace. I don't mean paying lip service to grace, I mean the real thing. The kind that looks sexual sin in the eye and says, 'this too is covered by the love of Jesus.' All of it. Your precious kids are going to make mistakes in expressing their sexuality. Just like you did, and do. Some of their decisions will absolutely break your heart."

Both Maria and William shifted in their seats, subconsciously acknowledging the truth of this statement.

"Read Matthew 25," Lou continued. "Jesus' followers asked him what it is going to be like when he comes back. After telling them to be ready and productive with the lives they have been given, he tells them that when he comes back, he's going to have some questions for everyone.[13] As Matthew writes it, our sex lives or desires will not be part of that conversation. Jesus will be primarily interested in how we loved the needy around us. Now, this is just one parable, of course. There are plenty of indications that our sexuality is a consideration in our salvation. However, it sometimes feels like we Christians have all agreed that sexual sin is the very worst variety of sin there is and that it will be the first thing on our report card when we meet Jesus."

"Yeah, that sounds about right," Maria said.

"That implicit idea, that sexual sin is something bigger and worse than other sins, is what makes us so judgmental about people's failures or differences in sexuality. Our response to sexual sin should be the same as we would give to any other sin – that this too is covered by the love and the blood of Jesus. Your family needs to be a place where sexual sin is met with an unrelenting, unflinching grace. Churches should be this way too."

"That's a good word right there, Lou," William said, nodding.

"Just one more thing that every Christian should keep in mind," Lou continued. "The church is the absolute best place for sinful people like you, me, and your kids. Christian faith always comes back to loving God with all your heart and loving other people well.[14] There is a lot talked about these days regarding the LGBT community.[15] There are complicated arguments to be understood regarding the relationship between non-traditional views of sexuality and Christian faith – much more complicated than we have historically realized or acknowledged. I'll tell you this though, Jesus wants everyone on the planet who is concerned with loving God with all their being, and loving others, to be in church. If this should ever come up with your kids or folks in your church, remember this – God wants believers connected to his body. The Spirit will help every person work out their salvation, but God's people should want everyone who is genuinely seeking God and trying to love others in their midst."[16]

Maria and William, both somewhat shell-shocked, sat in silence for a few moments before Maria said, "Wow, Grandpa! That's a lot to digest…and each little bit of it demands more conversation and thought."

"I know, but if you start thinking about these things and talking about them now, you have time to tackle them in small slices. You are already in the process of clarifying which values are going to be central to your conversations with your kids. You do not need to learn everything about every topic today and you certainly don't need to talk to Kayla and Andrew about all of them right now. Start intentionally working on your theological moorings today. Some will probably just need to be stated and affirmed. Others will require a lot more work. You can look for answers to specific questions over time, while ensuring that concepts like a positive view of sexuality and relentless grace are always at the center of your interactions with the kids."

"Grandpa, thank you so much for your time and your wisdom. It means a lot to us," Maria said as she started to clear the plate of cookies and the now empty coffee cups.

"Nonsense, dear. There's nothing I like more than talking with you – especially about genuinely important topics. I certainly hope that, in all my years, I've picked up at least a few things that can be useful to young folks like you."

Chuckling, William said, "Oh, it is definitely helpful. I'm just wondering how Maria is going to squeeze all of this onto her list."

"Me too," Maria said as she walked into the kitchen.

That evening, after the kids were in bed for the third time, Maria and William gathered at the kitchen table. William had made hot cups of tea for each of them and placed a brand new, impeccably sharp pencil on the table alongside their growing list of essentials in communicating with their children about sexuality.

Pulling out a chair to sit down, Maria remarked, "Wow! What a pencil!"

"I figured you would need a fresh one after our talk with Grandpa Lou. That was a lot to assimilate."

"It sure was. I have pages of notes from today. But, I think I have an idea of what we can put on the list so that we capture the key concepts," Maria said, still admiring the tip on the pencil.

"Well, don't keep me in suspense. Oh, and, don't keep me awake any longer than necessary," William said with an exhausted smile. "Grandpa wore my brain out today."

With that, Maria squared the paper up in front of her and wrote:

GOOD NEWS

"Good news, huh?" William asked. "Tell me more about why you chose that title."

"I've been overthinking about it," Maria said, winking at William. "I believe what Grandpa described is what we might label as a redemptive view of sexuality. It's a positive and good part of God's creation. We should understand that our bodies, sexuality, and intercourse are more than items on a long list of prohibitions. They are central features in God's design for our best possible lives."

"Sure," William agreed. "That's a pretty good word. So, what comes beneath the heading?"

"OK," said Maria. "Here's what I have." With that, she wrote the first statement.

GOOD NEWS

1. We view sexuality and our bodies as central to God's good creation.

"Wow, that's a long one," William observed.

With a slightly apologetic grin Maria replied, "I know, but I couldn't think of a short way to say it and I definitely did not want to end up with four commitments on this list and three on all the others."

"Sure. That would be stressful," William said with genuine empathy.

"You're not kidding," Maria sighed. "I went with the lesser of two evils – a long statement, but uniformity with the other list."

"Good choice," William responded with a slightly patronizing nod.

"Seriously though," Maria began. "What Lou said really struck home. We have a ton to learn and remember about all this, but we should at least commit to start down this road with our kids, assuring them that their bodies and their sexuality are good and intentional and valuable to God."

"I agree," William said nodding. "I never want our kids to believe that their bodies are bad, or dirty, or that their sexuality is gross. I would hate that for them."

"Exactly. We cannot lose sight of the fact that with sin in the world, our bodies and sexuality are under attack, just like everything else. Let's start with the beauty and purpose God intended when he designed human bodies, and our kids' bodies in particular."

"Preach!" William said, raising his right hand in a mock-worship gesture.

"Well," Maria smiled, "I can't help it. This is getting very real. If we can't help our kids understand that their physical bodies and their sexuality are intended for good, we just fall into the same old cycle of trying to scare them into or out of various behaviors. That has not led previous generations to healthy views of sexuality, so let's not repeat it hoping for a different outcome."

William began to speak, but Maria cut him off. "And if you say anything about that being the definition of insanity, I'll pour my tea in your lap."

After a moment's pause, William shook his head slightly, held back a smile, and said, "No, I was just going to say…how pretty you are."

Maria leaned over and kissed him on the cheek. "That's what I figured. Now let's move on," she said, returning to the paper in front of her and writing the second commitment on the list.

GOOD NEWS

1. We view sexuality and our bodies as central to God's good creation.
2. We value all phases of life.

"Huh," William said, staring at the page. "That seems deep and important…but I am not sure I am clear about what you have in mind here. Talk me through it."

"I know," Maria said, somewhat sheepishly. "I can't quite get it to say what I want it to say."

"Which is, what?"

"Well, it's all that stuff Grandpa Lou said about recognizing the opportunity for our kids to live out their sexuality in vibrant ways through the different stages of life. I want us to value and honor marriage, certainly our marriage. But, I also want to help our kids understand that sexuality is more than just making babies when you get married. I want them to value their time as teenagers. I want them to be comfortable as single people for whatever length of time they are. You know what I'm getting at?"

"Right, that was good stuff. I especially want the kids to understand that they do not need another person to complete them – that only God can give them a genuine sense of wholeness."[17]

"Yes," Maria said. "I want to help them recognize the value and the good in going through puberty, in starting to feel attracted to other people, in being single, and in getting married – if that happens. I want Kayla to believe it is beautiful to be a woman. I wonder if there is anything out there on something like how menstruation is a holy process."[18]

"Wow," William said, his face reddening a little. "You are really picking up on this, 'say things out loud,' vibe, aren't you?"

"Hey, it won't be long before Kayla starts her period. Get used to talking about it, buddy."

"Baby steps," William said, exhaling loudly. "I'm getting there. I've already said more words about sexuality in the last week than in my entire life before that. Give it some time."

"I know. I said, 'menstruating' mostly to freak you out," Maria said with a playful smile. "Forget about that for a minute."

"Done!"

"What do you think about the way I have this one stated on the list? Is there a better way to say it?"

After a moment's consideration, William offered, "What about something like, 'We honor sexuality in every phase of life'?"

"Hey, I like that!" Maria exclaimed. "That states it a little more accurately."

"Good. We can always wordsmith it more later. I imagine we will keep adjusting these lists as we move forward."

"Great! Then let's wrap this up and get to bed. My brain is exhausted from today," Maria said, picking up her pencil. She changed the wording on the second commitment to reflect William's updated version, then began the final entry to the list.

GOOD NEWS

1. We view sexuality and our bodies as central to God's good creation.
2. We honor sexuality in every phase of life.
3. We offer unflinching grace.

"Yes!" William said enthusiastically. "That one for sure! They are going to make mistakes. They will probably make decisions we wish they wouldn't and develop some beliefs that differ from ours. But, we will always offer them grace." His voice cracking just a little.

"Aw, sweetie! I like this passionate side of you," Maria said, leaning her head on William's shoulder.

"This one really gets me going," William said, clearing his throat slightly. "No matter what, I want our kids to know that they cannot do anything to make us stop loving them. That is not a question that should ever even cross their minds. This even goes beyond the sexuality issue. It's all of life. But, sexuality is probably where they will most worry that we might not forgive them."

"Well, there is not much I can add to that. Except, 'Amen!'" Maria said, raising her hands in the air. "Now, let's get to bed. It's been quite a day."

"You got it," William said as he stood up from his chair. "You go ahead, I'll straighten up in here."

"Thanks, babe." Then, taking hold of William's hand, Maria said, "I love you. This is a crazy journey we're going

on, but I can already tell it will make us stronger together."
She gave his hand a quick squeeze, then headed down the
hall toward their bedroom, just in time to see Andrew's
little head poking out from his bedroom door.

NOTES:

1. I once interviewed a young man not really named
Derek. When I asked him to give advice to parents and
church leaders on teaching young people topics of sexuality, he said, "Saying, 'Don't do it!' is fine in church, but it's
not a strong enough deterrent when you're alone with a
girl. Teach kids the positive purpose of sexuality – the ide-
als, not just the negative stuff." His point was well-taken.
Positive images of what sex and sexuality can be - the invitation into God's beautiful design for them – this is a much
stronger motivation than fear of sin and punishment. Ultimately, all sexual sin results in missing out on the best version of life possible, not just making God angry or poten-
tially getting pregnant. Form the habit of emphasizing the
positive "why" as you discuss behavioral standards.

2. I do not know of any science to back it up, but I
firmly believe that cookies make difficult conversations
qualitatively better and more productive.

3. We must choose our words carefully as we speak
of sexuality. When the word *sex* is used as a stand-in for
sexuality, we risk reducing sexuality to that one action. As
pointed out in Chapter 1, sexuality is an umbrella term

that includes biology, attraction, self-image, behavior, and more. Be as specific as possible when you use the word sex so that it refers either to intercourse or biological sex. Use the word sexuality to refer to the broader range of topics.

4. Genesis 1:27. To be sure, there is much to be questioned and discussed around gender (a person's understanding of their own status as male, female, or a non-binary option). We cannot work through those discussions here, but the positive proclamation of this little bit of Scripture is that the presence of male and female matters to God in terms of image-bearing. The biological sexes express the image of God in ways that intertwine and enhance each other.

5. For a robust discussion of gender and transgenderism, see Mark Yarhouse's work, *Understanding Gender Dysphoria*. Yarhouse does a fabulous job of distinguishing between the varied understandings of gender and the growing vocabulary used to describe them. He offers a window into the body of research in this area, as well as some practical ideas concerning how Christian people might respond to our friends and family in the gender dysphoric and transgender communities.

Yarhouse, Mark. *Understanding Gender Dysphoria: Navigating Transgender Issues in a Changing Culture.* Downers Grove: IVP Academic, 2015.

6. Genesis 1:26, 28. I certainly do not want to give the impression that sexual intercourse exists exclusively for

procreation. However, it should be celebrated that intercourse holds an honored and integral place in the creation plan. Sex is a vital component of God's good plan for us as partners in his ongoing creation work. It is included in God's declaration of, "Very good."

7. Genesis 3:17. Childbearing was originally a much less painful process, apparently. This text also explains that the presence of sin in the world is the source of centuries of sex and power being intertwined in unhealthy and destructive ways.

8. Specifically, Genesis 2:23.

9. Genesis 2:24. This is one of a thousand subtly, "woman-positive" texts in the Bible. Like most of them, when we read it with 21st century eyes it seems innocuous. But, nearly every culture in the ancient near east considered women to be the property of men. When they were married, a woman joined the man in his father's household. God's statement that the couple should leave their previous homes and start a new one of their own shows a valuing of women that was lightyears ahead of cultural norms. It implied that the wife was a full partner in the marriage, not a possession. The home established was a new creation in which the husband and wife would together express the image of God. This was revolutionary, which was probably why even the Israelites did not seem to pick up on it.

10. This is part of the story of my marriage and, as I have come to find out over the years, thousands of others'.

It is very difficult to grow up believing that having intercourse is the worst thing you could possibly do and that your body is something to be ashamed of, then flip a switch on your wedding night and feel great about being naked with your spouse. This led us (at 20 and 21 years old, respectively) to sex therapy. Sex therapy! If you ever want to plumb the depths of awkward newlywed conversations, I commend sex therapy to you. It did help us out quite a lot though, so we praise God for the awkwardness.

11. Most churches' implicit message is that normal people are married and have kids and if you are not married, you surely want to end up that way. With the age of marriage creeping up over 30 years old in the U.S., and the onset of puberty dropping below 10 years old in many cases, the average young person will be single for around 20 years between the onset of puberty and marriage. Some will be single permanently. Many will be single again, post-divorce. Parents and churches need to offer a positive vision for life as a single person. Here is a relatively recent article on the continuing trend of earlier onset of puberty:

http://health.usnews.com/health-news/health-wellness/articles/2015/04/17/why-kids-are-hitting-puberty-earlier-than-ever

12. 1 Corinthians 7:8.

13. Matthew 25 contains three parables that Jesus uses to describe what it will be like when he returns in the end. We usually refer to 25:1-13 as the parable of the virgins.

The point of this parable is that we do not know when he will return, so we need to be ready now, as well as prepared for it to be a while. 25:14-30 is the parable of the bags of gold – often called talents (an ancient measurement of money). Jesus will not be satisfied with a life that is lived out with the intention of not messing up too badly and thus getting kicked out of heaven. He will demand that we bear fruit in our lives – make something more from the life we are given. The parable of the sheep and the goats is found in 25:31-46. Jesus is most concerned about our heart for loving the world. His first question will be something like, "Did you feed me, clothe me, or care for me?" not, "Did you have sex with the wrong person?" This is not to say that sexuality is not a huge concern in Christian living. It obviously is. However, it is not the litmus test for salvation that we sometimes make it out to be either.

14. Matthew 22:34-40. While we cannot be reductionists about Christian faith, this statement is intentionally simple, and straight from Jesus's own mouth. Offering our whole being to God and in service of others is the ultimate metric of Christian life. If people agree on the centrality of these two great commands, they should be able to press in toward God together. Discussions of sexual ethics quickly devolve into moralizing about certain behaviors when they are not anchored in love for God and others. Such conversations will likely never move toward redemptive relationships.

15. I use the initials LGBT throughout the book. There are other initials, such as Q, I, A, etc. that are often included as well. I have chosen to use LGBT as it seems to be the standard in research and formal writing. LGBT presumably includes all non-traditional and non-binary views of sexuality. The decision to leave off other letters is in no way a matter of disrespect or disregard for people that identify themselves within those categories.

16. Read the descriptions of the Spirit's work in the Gospel of John, chapters 14-16. Jesus promises that, among other things, the Spirit will guide us toward truth and righteousness. This is a promise for all believers and for the Church community. I believe one of the great challenges of the 21st century will be the extent to which churches trust the work and leading of the Spirit when it comes to the growing spectrum of views on sexuality. This will require local churches and denominational leaders to wrestle with how they can invite LGBT people into their spaces and give the Spirit room to work in the hearts and minds of all parties involved.

17. With all due respect to *Jerry Maguire*, the idea that one person completes another has huge problems. On a relational level, it asks something of another person that is impossible. Namely, that they be fully themselves, plus a percentage of someone else. No one can be more than one person, and it is not fair to ask someone to try. On a theological level, taking a view that someone else makes

us complete makes an idol of a human by putting them in the position that only God should fill – only he can bring fulfillment to humans. He designed us that way. If you are interested in a beautiful theological treatment of this built-in desire, go here:

Coakley, Sarah. *God, Sexuality, and the Self: An Essay on 'The Trinity'*. Cambridge: Cambridge University Press, 2013.

18. No one has ever said greater things about the holy journey of female sexuality than Lisa Graham McMinn. She has great things to say about male sexuality as well.

McMinn, Lisa Graham. *Sexuality and Holy Longing: Embracing Intimacy in a Broken World*. San Francisco: Jossey-Bass, 2004.

WIDENING THE CIRCLE

"**YOU READY FOR** this?" Maria asked, giving William's hand a quick squeeze.

"I doubt it," he replied. "But we haven't let that stop us so far, have we?"

"It'll be fun." Maria said encouragingly.

As they spoke, the first few people started to trickle into the parenting class William and Maria were teaching at their church. Neither had ever taught a church class before, nor would they have believed a couple years previously that they ever would. But, things had changed a lot since then. Following their conversations with Anita, Bailey, Duane, and Grandpa Lou, Maria and William began to slowly implement the ideas collected on their list, which

Maria had eventually typed and color-coded. Two years down the road, they now found themselves coming to the end of the six-week course they had been teaching. They dedicated the first week to making the case for the necessity of parents' communicating about sexuality with their children. The next four weeks were spent covering each of the four categories of "The List" (as it was affectionately known to the class members). They intended to use their final session for discussion and questions.

"Welcome everyone," Maria said, bringing the room to order and pausing a moment to allow participants to find their seats. "We're going to get started," she continued. "It's our last session together, and as we promised last week, we want to use this morning for answering your questions."

"Yes," William picked up. "As we've told you, we are only a couple years into this ourselves and our oldest child has barely even started puberty. We are by no means experts, but expertise is not really the point. Creating space for our kids to be comfortable talking about some of the most challenging parts of growing up is the real end game. As an example, two years ago, I would never have been able to say that my daughter has started puberty with a straight face. So, I'm growing!" he concluded, with a look of exaggerated pride.

Poking him with her elbow slightly, Maria said, "That's right. I'm here to tell you that if this guy can grow into a man whose children talk to him about their penis and vagina and how babies are really made, then anyone can do it. And, of course, we hope that you *will* do it. As we all know, our kids live in a world that is utterly saturated with sexual messaging and images. Sticking our heads in the sand and hoping they pick up on some vague sense of a Christian sexual ethic is simply not good enough. It didn't work for previous generations of parents, and it certainly will not work for us as we raise kids in the world of screens and social media. So, today we will practice what we've been preaching. We invite you to ask any questions you would like. William and I will try answer them but, as you now know, it's OK if we don't have a simple answer. Perhaps someone else in the room will have wisdom to share. If not, we all must get comfortable doing the best we can and being transparent when we need to seek further information or insight."

"Well, I have a question that's been burning inside of me," a man to Maria's left chimed in. "We appreciate you guys sharing your story, but I want to know if you ever actually told Kayla what sex is!"

Laughing, William began, "Oh, right! Yes, we did. We had that conversation with her a day or two after we talked to Grandpa Lou. The funny thing is, she didn't even remember asking about it."

"Yes," Maria joined in. "But that's good in a way. She did not think it was a big deal at the time. A lot of other questions have come up in the past couple years and I genuinely believe that answering that first one, when it was pretty low-risk in terms of her concern about the topic, set the table for the more serious questions that have followed. I am certain that God led us into these conversations just in time to get started down this road, ahead of questions that she was much more invested in." Pointing to a woman directly in front of her, Maria said, "Brittany, you looked like you had a question a second ago."

"Oh, sure. I guess what I would like to know is, when did Kayla or Andrew, ask you a question that you did not have an answer to and how did that play out?"

Looking at Maria in confirmation, William said, "I think I can answer this one."

Smiling broadly, Maria said, "I was hoping you would, because I know exactly what you're going to say."

"Yes, you do. About a month ago Kayla and I were at the grocery store, in the checkout line. And, of course, there are all the crazy tabloids in the magazine rack as you wait. One of them featured a headline about celebrities considering gender transitions. Kayla was looking it, then turned to me and very loudly asked, 'Why would someone want to change from being a girl to being a boy?' I was a little caught off guard, especially because the lady in line behind us looked at me with a, 'She's got you now, Sucker!' grin on her face. I honestly wasn't sure what to say. Do I talk to her about gender dysphoria and non-binary under-standings of sexuality right there in the grocery store? Do

I answer it pragmatically? Or, theologically? And, by the way, I don't really have a great theological answer to give for that question, so that's a problem. I'll be honest with you, I punted a little. I told her we would be better off talking about it when we got home. Fortunately for me, it was time to pay for our groceries, so I did that and we left."

"When we got in the car," William continued, "I felt guilty about putting her off. Frankly, I hoped I could make it home and hand her off to Maria – a momentary lapse in courage, I admit. As we drove home, I knew I could not wait. I told Kayla that she asked a challenging question. Of course, I also repeated our motto: 'Mom and Dad love hard questions!' I apologized for delaying and told her I honestly needed a minute to think about it. I asked her what she knew about the topic of gender transition and people who become unhappy with their biological sex. Technically, I suppose I never answered the exact question she asked be-cause the conversation went a different direction. She was not actually reacting to the tabloid headline. It turned out that a classmate of hers had made some comments about wanting to transition her gender. The tabloid just remind-ed Kayla that she had been wanting to ask us about it. She doesn't know exactly what to make of the things her class-mate is saying. So, we ended up discussing her treatment of that young lady as child of God and reassuring Kayla that she could and should still be friends with that girl and try to understand how she is feeling. That's what she really wanted to discuss," William concluded.

"That is a good example," Maria jumped in, "Of what we call, 'communicating for meaning'. Kayla asked a question whose answer did not really matter to her. She was actually trying to understand how to respond to, and be in relationship with, a classmate. William engaged in a conversation with her, with the goal of helping her feel as though she had made meaning of something important in her life. Kayla could not even articulate what that thing was when the conversation began. If William had given her a definition of transgenderism, or a book, or just put her off, she would still be trying to make sense of the incredibly complex intersection of social relationships and different ideas about sexuality. Or worse, she would be asking friends or Siri."

"Yes, and that is exactly what we have learned in this process," William said. "Conversations often start with a question about something kids have heard in school or seen on television, but later they turn toward truly important parts of being human. And our oldest is just turning ten! I can't imagine where these conversations will take us as they grow older. I will tell you this, though – I'm so thankful that we are forming relationships with them now that will allow us to be part of conversations that will come in their teens and twenties. It's like the time we are spending with them today is earning us the right to be in the game when those years come along."

Another father in the audience spoke up saying, "I love all this, I really do. I guess I'm still unsure about what I do when my son asks about gender dysphoria or some sex position I've never even heard of."

"We totally understand that," Maria replied. "We feel that same fear. We try to read more and be proactive in increasing our own knowledge. But, the fact is that there will always be topics that we just do not have insight into. Think about the utter explosion of vocabulary our culture has started using to describe gender and sexual preference. Maybe those words existed ten years ago, but they were not part of the news broadcast at night or in every movie and television show that you watch. Even keeping up with that is a big job."

"I'm going to share what this has done for me," William added. "It has made me humble. I had to give up the notion that I can have all the answers. I've had to make peace with the fact that I sometimes must look something up before I can answer my kids' questions…and I'm sure that will increase exponentially as they get older. But, I have also become one hundred percent convinced that this is the exact right place to be." Pausing for a moment to fight back a tear, William continued, "Humbly, with a great deal of uncertainty, walking alongside our kids as they explore the world of sexuality in their own bodies and in the culture in which we live. The alternative is that they wander around out there by themselves and I will absolutely not allow that to happen."

Looking directly at the man that had asked the question, William continued, "I know that does not give you a concrete answer. The closest I could come to doing that is to say, do your best. I know that sounds trite, but what else can you do, really? Encourage your kids to ask questions and humbly do your best to answer them, while reserving the right to revisit a topic if you need to do some research. Be honest. Be humble. Make your kids' well-being more important than your feeling of competence. It is very challenging, but it is also deeply rewarding."

The room was quiet for a moment as everyone absorbed that exchange. A few more questions were asked and a decidedly lighthearted feel soon returned to the room. As the time approached for the class to wrap up, Maria picked up a stack of papers and said, "We've put together a little worksheet for you, so you can make your very own version of The List." Everyone chuckled a bit at this. "We filled in our own list, but also included some extra questions and space for you to add to it. After all, it is very possible that you have some circumstance in your life or your children's lives that requires some other considerations. We hope you will fill them out and make it a discipline to review them once a year. This will help you hold yourselves accountable for following through, and for updating your list as your kids grow up. It is no magic formula, but it is a starting place and means of being intentional."

Stepping forward, William said, "Before we finish, I would like to pray for us all. This is important and difficult work, but it is holy work. If you are a parent, you were called specifically to this." With that, he bowed his head and began to pray.

"Holy Father, we are so thankful for the honor of being parents. It is exhausting and glorious work. Give us the courage and the energy to walk alongside our kids as they navigate the wilds of sexuality – in their own bodies and in the world around them. Give us wisdom to know when to initiate conversations ourselves and skill to work through any question with our kids. We commit right now that we will be the ones to lead them forward. We will take on the awkward conversations, the humility that comes from not having all the answers, and the utter exhaustion of never going off-duty. We recognize the sacred gift it is to be parents and we declare that we will do everything in our power to guard and shepherd our little ones. As you never abandon us, we will not abandon them to wrestle with these enormous questions on their own. Amen."

YOUR LIST

THIS IS A book is called *We Need to Talk*. This is not just clever wordsmithing, it is my true appeal to you. So far, I have been doing all the talking, but now it is your turn - and this, my friends, was the point all along. Your family. Your kids. Your school. Your church. They are the point. They need to be places for conversations that lead to healthy, redemptive understandings about sexuality. So now my good readers, please sit somewhere comfortable, pour yourself the relaxing beverage of your choice, and take a few minutes to work through the questions below. They are designed to help you start right now with your plan to create an environment where you can talk about sexuality in positive, life-giving ways. May God bless you and those you love as you journey forward, and may we together turn the tide of Christians who have been too quiet for too long about God's good gift of sexuality.

RELATIONSHIPS

1. We are proactive.
2. We communicate for meaning.
3. We "walk along the way."
4. _____

(Is there anything unique to your life, environment, or family that needs to be included on this list?)

What is the next step for you?

- A commitment to speaking about bodies as perfectly normal parts of life?
- A conversation with your kids about changing the way you speak at home (i.e. using anatomical names for body parts)?
- A trip to the bookstore for a resource or two?[1]
- Something else?

Use the space below to describe how you might change the way you relate to your children and/or to other people in your environment.

HONESTY
1. We love hard questions!
2. We practice mutual vulnerability.
3. Girls get to talk too.
4. _____

What is the next step for you?
- Figure out how to encourage more questions?
- Find a way to pose some of them yourself?
- Share some of your own experiences?
- Something else?

Use the space below to describe how you might open your lives and environment to more honest conversation about relationships, our bodies, and other topics of sexuality.

THE PROGRAM

1. We have a team.
2. We have consistent messaging.
3. We have consistent practices.
4. _____

What is the next step for you?

- Consider who you invite to be on your team? Invite them?
- Describe the most important ideas you want your kids to remember?
- Decide what practices to put into your life that will help encourage conversation and keep your most important values in front of your kids?

Use the space below to describe what you envision your Program looking like when it is running at full steam.

GOOD NEWS

1. We view sexuality and our bodies as central to God's good creation.
2. We honor sexuality in every phase of life.
3. We offer unflinching grace.
4. _____

What is the next step for you?

- Read up on the centrality of sexuality to human experience and God's creation?[2]
- Find ways (vocabulary and practices) to describe your child's current phase of life and sexuality as honorable and good?
- Have conversation assuring your kids that grace is always offered at home?[3]
- Something else?

Use the space below to describe how you will work to make your home, church, or school an environment where sexuality is understood as positive and valuable, even when mistakes are made.

NOTES:

1. There are six zillion books and curriculums available to help you understand sexuality well and to share it with your kids. I have certainly not read them all and I am sure there are other valuable resources out there. Here are a few of my favorites, specifically for your own education and for helping educate your kids.

Burns, Jim. *God Made Your Body*. Pure Foundations Series. Bloomington, MN: Bethany House Publishers, 2009.

This is one of a series of little books that Jim has written to help parents talk about sexuality with kids from early childhood forward.

McKee, Jonathan. *More Than Just the Talk: Becoming Your Kids' Go-To Person About Sex*. Bloomington, MN: Bethany House Publishers, 2015.

For those who want guidance in what actual words to say to your kids as you talk about sexuality. Also, a good way to take another step toward speaking explicitly about sexuality, which McKee certainly does.

Parrot, Les and Leslie. *Real Relationships: From Bad to Better and Good to Great*. Grand Rapids: Zondervan, 2011.

In a world in which I had absolute power, I would make this required reading for all young people and those that love them. It covers everything from the innate desire to connect to God, to friends, dating, breaking up, physical intimacy, and sex. It also includes workbook material with each chapter.

2. Here are some fabulous resources to understand sexuality and its place in God's creation. Each of them is worth every moment of your time. Others have been mentioned in previous end notes, so if you have not seen them, make sure you do.

Bell, Rob. *Sex God: Exploring the Endless Connections Between Sexuality and Spirituality*. New York: Harper Collins, 2012.

This is a down-to-earth, broad-based, and inspiring theology of sexuality. A perfect entry-level discussion of God's purpose for sexuality that will stretch your definition and awareness of the topic.

Hirsch, Debra. *Redeeming Sex: Naked Conversations About Sexuality and Spirituality*. Downers Grove: IVP Books, 2105.

This book is raw and gritty, but Hirsch does a relatively thorough job addressing major social and theological issues in sexuality.

Winner, Lauren. *Real Sex: The Naked Truth About Chastity*. Grand Rapids: Brazos Press, 2005.

Winner mingles her own experience as a single woman together with theological and spiritual truth about sexuality in general, and singleness specifically.

3. Every seminar I have ever conducted and nearly every conversation I have had with teens and college students ends up at some version of this question: "How can Christians understand LGBT and transgender issues?" The answers are not simple, but these resources will help if you are interested in going deeper.

Yuan, Christopher and Angela. *Out of a Far Country: A Gay Son's Journey to God. A Broken Mother's Search for Hope.* Colorado Springs: Waterbrook Press, 2011.

This is the joint memoir of a young man and mother as they navigate his same sex attraction and depression as a Christian family with a historical interpretation of homosexuality in the Bible.

Marin, Andrew. *Us vs. Us: The Untold Story of Religion and the LGBT Community.* Colorado Springs: NavPress, 2016.

This is Marin's second book. I would highly recommend *Love Is an Orientation*, his first book as well. *Us vs. Us* is a readable and compelling description of the largest survey ever done on faith in the LGBT community.

Sprinkle, Preston and Gundy, Stanley N. *Two Views on Homosexuality, the Bible, and the Church.*

Preston Sprinkle and Stanley N. Grundy are the editors of this unique book that convenes a conversation between four great scholars (William Loader, Megan K. DeFranza, Wesley Hill, and Stephen R. Holmes). Each of them offers an essay on issues of homosexuality, biblical interpretation, ethics, and the reaction of the church to the LGBT community. Each essay includes reactions from the other three scholars. This is a robust introduction to the thinking of evangelical Christians who view the issue of homosexual relationships from both the "traditional" and "affirming" sides of the aisle. This book will challenge every reader.

ORDER INFORMATION

To order additional copies of this book, please visit
www.redemption-press.com.
Also available on Amazon.com and BarnesandNoble.com
Or by calling toll free 1-844-2REDEEM.

CPSIA information can be obtained
at www.ICGtesting.com
Printed in the USA
FFOW01n0251100418
46223120-47543FF

9 781683 145073